100
Best Bible
Verses
to
Overcome
Worry
& Anxiety

100

Best Bible
Verses
to
Overcome
Worry
& Anxiety

BETHANYHOUSE

a division of Baker Publishing Group
Minneapolis, Minnesota

© 2021 by Bethany House Publishers

Published by Bethany House Publishers
11400 Hampshire Avenue South
Bloomington, Minnesota 55438
www.bethanyhouse.com

Bethany House Publishers is a division of
Baker Publishing Group, Grand Rapids, Michigan

Library of Congress Cataloging-in-Publication Data
Description: Minneapolis, Minnesota : Bethany House, a division of Baker
    Publishing Group, [2021] | Includes bibliographical references.
Identifiers: LCCN 2020058111 | ISBN 9780764239052 (casebound) | ISBN
    9780764238383 (trade paperback) | ISBN 9781493431656 (ebook)
Subjects: LCSH: Anxiety—Biblical teaching. | Worry—Biblical teaching. | Anxiety—
    Religious aspects—Christianity. | Worry—Religious aspects—Christianity. |
    Bible—Use.
Classification: LCC BV4908.5 .A15 2021 | DDC 248.8/6—dc23
LC record available at https://lccn.loc.gov/2020058111

Unless otherwise indicated, Scripture quotations are from THE HOLY BIBLE,
NEW INTERNATIONAL VERSION®, NIV® Copyright © 1973, 1978, 1984, 2011
by Biblica, Inc.® Used by permission. All rights reserved worldwide.

Scripture quotations labeled CSB have been taken from the Christian Standard
Bible®, copyright © 2017 by Holman Bible Publishers. Used by permission. Chris-
tian Standard Bible® and CSB® are federally registered trademarks of Holman
Bible Publishers.

Scripture quotations labeled ESV are from The Holy Bible, English Standard Ver-
sion® (ESV®), copyright © 2001 by Crossway, a publishing ministry of Good News
Publishers. Used by permission. All rights reserved. ESV Text Edition: 2016

Scripture quotations labeled GNT are from the Good News Translation in Today's English Version-Second Edition. Copyright © 1992 by American Bible Society. Used by
permission.

Scripture quotations labeled NASB are from the New American Standard Bible®
(NASB), Copyright © 1960, 1971, 1977, 1995, 2020 by The Lockman Foundation. All
rights reserved.

Scripture quotations labeled NLT are taken from the Holy Bible, New Living Translation, copyright © 1996, 2004, 2015 by Tyndale House Foundation. Used by permission of Tyndale House Publishers, Inc., Carol Stream, Illinois 60188. All rights
reserved.

Scripture quotations labeled NKJV are from the New King James Version®. Copyright
© 1982 by Thomas Nelson. Used by permission. All rights reserved.

Scripture quotations identified The Passion Translation are from
The Passion Translation®. Copyright © 2017, 2018 by Passion
& Fire Ministries, Inc. Used by permission. All rights reserved.
ThePassionTranslation.com.

Scripture quotations labeled KJV are from the King James Version
of the Bible

Cover design by Brand Navigation

21 22 23 24 25 26 27   7 6 5 4 3 2 1

> # "Cast all your anxiety on him because he cares for you."
>
> ## 1 PETER 5:7

CONTEXT

In this short letter, Peter gives Christians hope in the midst of unjust suffering. He tells the recipients of his letter that his message is intended to testify to the "true grace of God. Stand fast in it" (1 Peter 5:12).

MEANING

If we are to "stand fast" in the true grace of God, what does that mean for us when we are going through a heart-pounding season of worry or anxiety?

First, let's turn back the clock and remember an important truth about Peter. He wasn't just a spectator to the life of Jesus. He walked with him. He learned from him. He ate with him. He walked on water toward him. Notoriously, he denied him. And ultimately, he was embraced and forgiven by him.

All that to say, Peter spent a lot of time observing Jesus during his earthly ministry. That means Peter had firsthand knowledge of how our Savior not only withstood suffering himself, but how he took on our suffering as well.

Peter witnessed Jesus' compassion for others. He saw Jesus cast out demons. And he could tell you some pretty fascinating stories about how Jesus calmed storms—not just the ones on the sea, but the ones on the inside of real souls.

That's the kind of storm-calming Jesus we find in today's verse—the one who takes our fears and anxieties upon himself. In fact, Peter reminds us that when we are worried, we can do more than simply take our concerns to the Lord. We can cast them upon him! In the Greek, *cast* means to hurl, throw, or fling. When we cast our anxiety on God, it doesn't mean all our worries disappear. But it does mean that God will carry the load for us—no matter what we throw at him.

Why would God do such a thing? Peter tells us why in today's verse: ". . . because he cares for you."

APPLICATION

Do you ever feel like you don't know where to go with your anxiety and your worries? Maybe you've had someone tell you that the answer to anxiety is to simply "stop worrying," as if anxious thoughts can be turned off with a switch.

But that's not how God operates.

God doesn't tell you to ignore your anxiety or to simply "stop worrying." He doesn't say there's something wrong with you if you have anxiety. He is saying, "Give it all to me. In fact, you can actually throw it all on me! Because I really do care about you."

ADDITIONAL READING

Psalm 55:22 • Matthew 6:25–30 • Isaiah 49:15

"Do not be anxious about anything,
but in every situation, by prayer
and petition, with thanksgiving,
present your requests to God.
And the peace of God, which
transcends all understanding,
will guard your hearts and
your minds in Christ Jesus."

PHILIPPIANS 4:6–7

CONTEXT

Philippians starts with a greeting from Paul to the church in Philippi, a prayer for "Grace and peace to you from God our Father and the Lord Jesus Christ." The book ends here with a reminder of that peace as bookends for some hard topics, like resisting false teachers and facing suffering. Since these letters were often read out loud to the whole church, Paul wanted these thoughts to be among the last words the believers heard.

MEANING

Every time a fear surfaces in our minds, we have two choices: dwell on our worry, or give it up to God in prayer. Paul tells us that trusting God with our anxiety is the better way, no matter what: "about anything" and "in every situation" covers

it all. There's no fear that you can't take to God to be re-
placed with his peace.

This peace isn't a general calm with no troubles. It's an ac-
tive peace; it "guards" both our hearts (emotions) and minds
(thoughts). That's military language, like the Psalms describing God as our defender and shield against enemies. When
we pray, we aren't just comforted; we're protected.

Besides that, God's peace "transcends all understanding."
Our human minds can't explain it or even fully grasp it. If
you've ever seen fellow believers choose to trust God in the
middle of terrible suffering and wondered how they were
able to do it, you've seen this amazing peace at work.

How can we know this is true? Just before this passage,
in verse 5, Paul reminds us, "The Lord is near." Not far off
in a distant heaven, blissfully unbothered by human troubles
and only able to be reached by a few super-spiritual people,
but "near." When we pray, God hears us, because he's always
close by.

APPLICATION

So often we believe it's up to us to be strong and fight anxiety. But here, Paul tells us that it is God who guards us and
gives us peace. Yes, we have a part to play, but it's not making
a list, gritting our teeth, and trying harder.

It's turning constantly to prayer in every moment of fear,
choosing to be thankful, and resting in the peace God gives
through Jesus. Challenge yourself to put this into practice by
praying short prayers for peace when your instinct is to worry
instead, and thank God for being close enough to hear and
loving enough to care.

ADDITIONAL READING

Psalm 97:10–11 • Psalm 145:18 • Ephesians 2:13

> ## "Come to me, all of you who are weary and burdened, and I will give you rest."
>
> MATTHEW 11:28 CSB

CONTEXT

These comforting words from Jesus, along with verses 29 and 30, are part of a passage in Matthew's Gospel known as the Great Invitation. Jesus was speaking to crowds of people in Galilee, and just before this passage, he denounced "the towns where most of his miracles were done, because they did not repent" (11:20). His strong words shifted to praising his Father in heaven and then addressing the burdens people felt trying to live by the Pharisees' rules. Today, we might not be weighed down by widespread legalism like in ancient days, but Christ extends his invitation to us—to come to him and find relief from the burden of sin and the pressures of life.

MEANING

Rather than an impersonal invitation, notice that Christ says, "Come to me." He is not inviting you to a program or a religion. He desires a personal relationship. He already knows everything about you, and now he invites you to believe and trust in him.

Jesus calls out to everyone who feels "weary and burdened." For most of us, that brings to mind physical exhaustion. And certainly, in our desire to maximize the twenty-four hours each day holds, it's common to feel tired. But Jesus also wants to help those of us who are tired mentally, emotionally, spiritually—the kind of weariness that can linger no matter how much rest and sleep we try to get.

Notice too that Christ promises to give you rest. He won't simply show or tell you how to rest. Again, he makes it personal and says, "I will give you rest."

APPLICATION

Life is complex. It's not always possible to pinpoint why we feel weary or under pressure. Other times, the source is clear, we just don't know how to fix it.

That's the beauty of Christ's Great Invitation. We don't need to know what's weighing us down; we just need to respond to his three simple yet powerful words: "Come to me. . . ."

Exodus 20:11 tells us, "The LORD made the heavens and the earth . . . then he rested on the seventh day" (CSB). So clearly, God values rest. Turn to him for the deep, lasting rest your body and soul need.

ADDITIONAL READING

1 Peter 5:7 • Proverbs 3:5 • Jeremiah 31:25

"But he said to me, 'My grace is sufficient for you, for my power is made perfect in weakness.' Therefore I will boast all the more gladly about my weaknesses, so that Christ's power may rest on me."

2 CORINTHIANS 12:9

CONTEXT

Second Corinthians is a letter written by Paul the apostle to the church at Corinth, which is in modern-day Greece. The themes of the letter include suffering, forgiveness, and generosity.

MEANING

In his second letter to the church of Corinth, Paul has a lot of hard things to say—hard both in the sense that they are difficult to understand as well as sometimes being unpleasant to hear. An example of the latter is that he admonishes the disciples for their divisiveness and defends himself as an apostle of Christ.

An example of the former type of "hard thing" is that in this chapter, he talks about "a man" who was "caught up into the third heaven." What does this mean? There is much debate, but most believe he is talking about a special revelation he himself had. From there, perhaps even more confusingly, he says that God gave him a "thorn in the flesh" so he wouldn't be conceited. What was that thorn? Again, there is much debate.

But regardless of what that thorn was, he goes on to say that he prayed for it to be taken away, but God refused. Instead, God said that his own strength was made perfect in weakness. This sounds discouraging at first, but in fact it's good news of God's power and grace. He may not answer our prayers the way we expect or even want, but he always turns bad things on their heads. He redeems things, making weaknesses strengths and overcoming evil with good. For this we can be thankful.

APPLICATION

Do you have a thorn in the flesh? Something that makes you feel weak or embarrassed? If so, take it to God and ask him to remove it. He may or he may not, but know that he will turn it around for your good and his glory.

ADDITIONAL READING

Genesis 50 • Isaiah 41:10

"The LORD is my shepherd,
I lack nothing."

CONTEXT

The Psalms are a collection of prayers and hymns written by David, Solomon, and several other ancient Israelites. Psalm 23, written by David, comes out of his experience as a shepherd in his youth. It is one of the most well-known passages in all of Scripture.

MEANING

This entire psalm paints a picture of you as a sheep and God as your good and loving shepherd. The Lord provides food and water, and also protects you from harm. There is a kind of harm that comes from our own ignorance or willfulness, like falling from a cliff or into deep water, but there's also the kind that comes from an enemy attack. God protects us from both of these, using his "rod and staff" to guide our steps as well as to ward off predators.

Seeing God as our shepherd is common in both the New and Old Testaments. And it makes sense. We are vulnerable and often simpleminded creatures, and we desperately need his watchful eye on us at all times. Jesus called himself the Good Shepherd, and promised that he would give his life for his sheep.

This first verse of Psalm 23 sets the stage with a short but powerful two-part statement. First, "the Lord is my shepherd." He's not just our shepherd. It's personal. We can often fall into the trap of thinking God loves us in general terms and forget that he loves each of us as individuals. As Jesus taught in a parable, he would leave the ninety-nine sheep for just one who was lost.

Next, the psalmist says, "I lack nothing." There is nothing you need that God hasn't provided. The same shepherd who would put himself in harm's way to protect you will also make sure you have exactly what you need to thrive.

APPLICATION

This psalm is often used to comfort the bereaved, and with good reason. It promises that God will be with us as we pass through the shadow of death. But we also need to consider what this psalm says to those worried about everyday things as well. You lack nothing! God will provide and protect. If he promises to be with us even in death—and showed it through the sacrifice of his own Son—he will also be with us in this life, leading you to the pastures and water you need to sustain and nourish you.

ADDITIONAL READING

John 10:11–18 • Luke 15:3–7

"Peace I leave with you; my peace I give you. I do not give to you as the world gives. Do not let your hearts be troubled and do not be afraid."

JOHN 14:27

CONTEXT

Jesus speaks these words to his disciples during his farewell discourse at the Last Supper. He is comforting his eleven remaining disciples and preparing them for his impending departure. Jesus announces his gift of peace just after promising the coming presence of the Holy Spirit in verse 26.

MEANING

Jesus tells his disciples what he is leaving them, or bestowing upon them, letting them know ahead of time the inheritance that lay in store: peace—more specifically, *his* peace.

It is an assured, foundational, and eternal peace that only Jesus could give because only he was able to accomplish it: "But he was pierced for our transgressions, he was crushed for our iniquities; the punishment that brought us peace was on him, and by his wounds we are healed" (Isaiah 53:5). It is "peace with God through our Lord Jesus Christ" (Romans 5:1).

It is not the peace of the world. While it was common for people of Jesus' day to speak or wish peace to one another in greeting and in farewell—sincerely or not—any peace given in the world is conditional and temporary. In contrast, not only did Jesus provide our peace, he is our peace (Ephesians 2:14).

Finally, knowing he will shortly finish the work of reconciling man to God, Jesus tells the disciples not to worry about or fear the earthly trials he knows will be coming their way.

APPLICATION

Jesus has given us his perfect peace. The world didn't give it to us, and the world can't take it away. It is ours. But we make choices every day about whether we "let the peace of Christ rule" in our hearts (Colossians 3:15) or give in to worry or fear. But how do we avoid sliding into anxiety, especially when someone or something in our world seems to be in danger?

Perhaps we should remind ourselves of the price Jesus paid for our peace.

And because we do have the peace of being reconciled to God, we can follow this directive found in Philippians 4:6–7: "Do not be anxious about anything, but in every situation, by prayer and petition, with thanksgiving, present your requests to God. And the peace of God, which transcends all understanding, will guard your hearts and your minds in Christ Jesus."

ADDITIONAL READING

Ephesians 2:14–18 • John 16:33

Isaiah 26:3 • Romans 5:1–2

> "But if we confess our sins to God, he will keep his promise and do what is right: he will forgive us our sins and purify us from all our wrongdoing."
>
> 1 JOHN 1:9 GNT

CONTEXT

The book of 1 John was written to encourage and assure people of the church after some began to drift from God's truth. Some leaders became false teachers who tried to convert others to their way of thinking. John wrote his letters to speak the truth about who Jesus is and why he came.

MEANING

In this portion of 1 John, John is talking about living in the light, which he describes as "having fellowship with one another" (1 John 1:7) and obeying God's Word (1 John 2:5). Notice how he says, "live in the light"; he doesn't say, "live perfectly." We tend to believe that it is our responsibility to make ourselves righteous before we can ever approach God. Unfortunately, there are still many today who teach this message; they use fear as a way to gain followers. This kind of thinking may come from a place of shame, a desire for control, or maybe a misunderstood view of God. Either way, John corrects this thinking by instructing us to live in fellowship with one another, pursuing righteousness not through works alone, but by the shed blood of Jesus Christ. He is the

only one who is righteous, and it is only through him that we
are made righteous.

APPLICATION

Walking in God's forgiveness and knowing that he holds you
in his hands is one of the greatest weapons that you have
against fear and worry. When we are living in the light, God
provides for our every need. If our every need is already
taken care of by our Father, what need is there for fear or
worry? I encourage you today, step into the light. Humbly
recognize your sin and your need for Jesus. Confess your
doubt and take him at his word. Begin to live a life where
you don't have to spend your days hiding parts of yourself
from God. God wants to forgive you, and he wants to lead
you. He wants to shift your focus from fear to faith, and from
worry to wonder. Will you trust him today?

ADDITIONAL READING

2 Corinthians 5:21 • John 14:27 • Joshua 1:9

> "For the wages of sin is death,
> but the gift of God is eternal life
> in Christ Jesus our Lord."
>
> ROMANS 6:23

CONTEXT

The book of Romans is a letter written by the apostle Paul
to the Christians living in Rome. Scholars believe he wrote
it from Corinth and had never visited Rome up to that point.
The main reason for the letter was to give the new believers
there a clear understanding of the basics of the Christian
faith, the gospel, and the Christian's identity and responsibilities in Christ.

MEANING

Romans chapter 6 is an explanation of how the Christian is
dead to sin through Christ's death on the cross; therefore,
we shouldn't let sin continue to rule over us. Now, in Christ,
we are set free from sin and are instead servants of God!
In other words, we used to work for sin, and received the
"wages," or payment, for our labors. This payment was death.

But now we are free of our old slavery to sin. We have a
new master, and now we serve God instead. But working for
God isn't just like swapping out one boss for another. We no
longer have to earn our wages, as if we're paying for our salvation through the good things we do for him. No, we could
never pay him back for what he's done for us. He bought our

freedom and salvation through the death of his beloved Son, which is of infinite value.

No, our salvation is not a result of earned wages. When God freed us from sin, he gave us a free gift—eternal life. This would have been impossible without Jesus Christ, who paid for our sins, clearing us of all debt.

We no longer have to live in shame and fear. We were bought by God and will live eternally with him! No matter what happens in this world, our future is secure.

APPLICATION

It's hard to think past this present life sometimes. Things weigh us down—finances, difficult relationships, health concerns. But all these things are temporary. We will outlive any and all of those problems, and through faith in Christ we have been given a free gift that overshadows any darkness or uncertainty we feel.

You are an eternally loved, eternally living being. Remind yourself of that every day!

ADDITIONAL READING

John 14:1–4 • Romans 8:18–21

> "Cast your burden on the LORD,
> and he will sustain you; he will never
> permit the righteous to be moved."
>
> PSALM 55:22 ESV

CONTEXT

David wrote Psalm 55 after he had been betrayed by his son, his counselor, and most of Israel. While he laments his difficult situation, he also calls out to God, knowing he is the Judge and the Father who sustains him fully.

MEANING

David is experiencing a lot of pain after being betrayed by his own son, Absalom. After learning that his counselor Ahithophel has sided with Absalom, David flees Jerusalem for fear of what Absalom may do to him and his servants. So much of David's life has been a chase. He's had to prove himself repeatedly to the people of Israel, and still, David probably feels like he's coming up short.

It seems like life would be easier if David crossed the Jordan, stayed out of Israel, and just let Absalom take over. After all, Absalom is next in line right now, so it seems like David could rest easy knowing he didn't have to be responsible for Israel anymore.

Of course, David doesn't take this route. He's devastated, yes. And his fear does drive him out of Israel temporarily, but David cries out to God in Psalm 55. He reminds himself, and us, to cast our burdens on the Lord. God knows who is righteous, and he sustains the righteous.

When God chose David to be king, he knew what lay ahead for him. Being chosen by God doesn't guarantee simplicity or ease. Throughout the Bible, we are shown that it actually guarantees the opposite. But the good news is this: You have full access to our savior. When you cast your burdens on him, he will be there to save you. The righteous will not be moved.

APPLICATION

Now that you know the context, reread Psalm 55. You probably haven't been betrayed as deeply as David, yet I'm sure you can relate to his pains. Commit verse 22 to memory over the next few days. When you feel your anxiety rising, repeat this verse to yourself, and let it bring you stillness.

ADDITIONAL READING

2 Samuel 22:7 • 1 Chronicles 22:19 • 1 Peter 5:7

> "But he was pierced for our transgressions, he was crushed for our iniquities; the punishment that brought us peace was on him, and by his wounds we are healed."
>
> ISAIAH 53:5

CONTEXT

Isaiah 53 speaks of the "suffering Messiah" and is one of the most famous passages of prophecy about Christ in the entire Bible. Not only does it foretell the manner of Christ's death, but it also spells out exactly why he had to die: for our sins.

MEANING

This chapter is one of the saddest but also one of the most hopeful in all of Scripture. It is heartbreakingly sad because it depicts the pain, loneliness, and suffering of our Lord and Savior. It even horrifyingly talks about how it was God's will to crush him. How can this be? The only explanation is sin.

Sin, our rebellion against God, is so utterly reprehensible that it must be punished. And yet God, in all three persons—Father, Son, and Holy Spirit—loves us so much that the Father was willing to punish the Son instead of us, and the Son was willing to bear it.

But this chapter is also hopeful. How valuable we must be to God for him to go through all this for us. Every one of us "like sheep has gone astray" (v. 6). But he loved us even in our wandering.

This verse tells us where peace and healing come from. They can't appear without a real acknowledgment of sin and a payment for that sin. They come, of course, from God's grace, shown through Christ's death on our behalf.

APPLICATION

Acknowledge how you've gone astray from the God who loved you. Repent of your wandering and come back to him. Then thank him for the brutal punishment he took on your behalf. It wasn't easy, but Jesus sees that you are worth it.

ADDITIONAL READING

2 Corinthians 5:21 • 1 Peter 2:24 • Hebrews 9:22

> "Jesus said to her, 'I am the resurrection and the life. The one who believes in me will live, even though they die.'"

> JOHN 11:25

CONTEXT

The book of John was written by the apostle John, one of Jesus' closest friends while on his earthly ministry. It is believed that this was the last of the Gospels to be written. In chapter 20, John states that the book was written "that you may believe that Jesus is the Messiah, the Son of God, and that by believing you may have life in his name" (v. 31).

MEANING

Lazarus, one of Jesus' friends and supporters, was dead. And now Lazarus's sister, Martha, was blaming Jesus for his death: "If you had been here, my brother would not have died" (John 11:21). Despite her sadness, even these seemingly bitter words were spoken in faith, as she followed it up with, "But I know that even now God will give you whatever you ask."

Jesus responds with comfort—not only for Martha but for all who believe. He is not just a miracle worker who can bring a decomposing body back from the dead for a while until it will inevitably die again. No, he is more than that. He IS the resurrection. He IS the life. And that means he can give life that lasts forever. Yes, our bodies will one day die, but we will rise again to be with our Savior for eternity. And not only us, but our loved ones who believe in Christ.

APPLICATION

But how can we know this to be true? What proof does he offer? First, we have the evidence of Lazarus himself. This miracle wasn't kept secret—Lazarus went on to live his life in public for all to see. Many came to faith, but for others it was the last straw. He was becoming too popular, so the Pharisees decided to kill him.

Which of course leads to the second proof: Jesus' own resurrection. He is too powerful to keep in a grave. He doesn't just have life—he IS life, and that life could not be overcome.

And that means there's hope! Hope that even when our bodies die, we will go on to live forever at his side, along with our loved ones who believed in Christ. His love and power are forever to all who call upon him. Is there any better news than this?

ADDITIONAL READING

John 10:28–30 • 2 Corinthians 4:18 • John 3:1–21

> "Then Jesus said to his disciples, 'Therefore I tell you, do not worry about your life, what you will eat; or about your body, what you will wear.'"
>
> Luke 12:22

CONTEXT

The Gospel of Luke was written by one of Jesus' disciples, Luke, to a man named Theophilus. Scholars debate whether Theophilus, which means "friend of God," was a living person or if Luke was writing to a pen name with the hope of reaching all Christians. In either case, the Gospel of Luke offers a detailed and warm retelling of the works of Jesus, and includes more parables than any other Gospel. Through Luke's writing, we see Jesus' insistence that the gospel is for everyone—Jews and Gentiles, rich and poor, male and female—and how it is truly good news for those who belong to God.

MEANING

Jesus spoke to his disciples about worry after telling the parable of the rich fool, who stored up wealth in his barns for safekeeping. The same fear that caused the rich man to hoard his wealth is the same fear Jesus' disciples may have faced—the fear of not having enough. The disciples probably realized at this point that following Jesus wasn't safe, and it wouldn't look at all like what their world considered comfortable, let alone successful.

The disciples aren't pursuing material things—they've committed their lives to pursuing Jesus, their Rabbi. And because they're committed to knowing, learning from, and following Jesus, Jesus himself offers reassurance that God knows and sees their real, practical needs: food, water, shelter, and clothing.

Jesus' command to not worry about physical needs is rooted in trust. Instead of chastising them for their anxiety, Jesus understands and reassures them that God sees them. God sees them, and they can trust him. In later verses, Jesus offers tangible reminders of all the other creatures God provides for: the birds and the lilies and the natural world.

APPLICATION

God knows you're doing your best to follow him, and sometimes this means making decisions that aren't focused on financial savvy or material gain. When worry and fear about not having enough arise, it's okay to be honest with God. He sees all your needs, right down to the most mundane ones.

Take a moment to reflect on all the ways God has provided for you in the past. By doing something tangible with your worry—making a list of things you're thankful for, or going on a walk and noting plants and animals—you can refocus your mind on what's true. If the God of heaven can care for lilies and birds so beautifully, surely the needs of your life are in good hands. Luke's Gospel shows us that believers can be assured that a God who cares about them will also care about their needs—especially their most basic ones—and hear their requests.

ADDITIONAL READING

Deuteronomy 8:4 • Matthew 6:25–34

> "The thief comes only to steal and kill and destroy. I have come that they may have life, and have it to the full."
>
> JOHN 10:10

CONTEXT

The first half of John 10 portrays Jesus as a Good Shepherd and his people as his sheep. In the second half of John 10, Jesus declares himself to be the Son of God, saying, "My sheep listen to my voice; I know them, and they follow me. I give them eternal life, and they shall never perish; no one will snatch them out of my hand" (vv. 27–28). This devotion focuses on the characterization of Jesus as our Shepherd and Savior.

MEANING

In biblical times, shepherds led their flocks to protected areas at night to rest. These areas were bordered by rocks or bushes, and shepherds slept at the entrance to guard the sheep against thieves and wild animals. John 10:1–21 illustrates Jesus as our Good Shepherd and us as his sheep. Like shepherds guarding their flocks, Jesus defends and protects us from harm.

Thieves come "only to steal and kill and destroy," but Jesus came to give us life and to give it abundantly. *Abundance* means extremely plentiful or overflowing fullness. The devil desires our destruction, but Jesus desires us to have abundant life. That includes a life free from anxiety and worry. If we spend our days fretting over what could go wrong, we allow a liar and a thief to steal, kill, and destroy the abundant life that Jesus died to give us.

However, with our Good Shepherd shielding us, we can take back abundant life. We are Jesus' sheep, and we can rest knowing that he'll defend and protect us against all harm. Let that knowledge restore your joy, security, and peace.

APPLICATION

You can move forward without worry, fear, anxiety, or obsessive thoughts about tomorrow. Jesus doesn't want you to barely survive or have destructive thoughts; he wants your life to be rich with peace, strength, freedom, courage, delight, and love. The next time you feel the thief clawing away your peace, remember you are held in the care of your Good Shepherd. He is watching over you to protect you from predators, including your own thoughts.

You are a precious sheep in Jesus' flock. He won't let you stray far from the protected area, and he will defend and shield you from harm. Ask the Lord to help you reclaim abundant life. Rebuke that thief in the name of Jesus and claim aloud that he has no power in your life. Memorize peaceful Scripture and recite it when tough moments come. Take every anxious thought captive and surrender it to Jesus.

ADDITIONAL READING

Exodus 14:14 • Joshua 1:9 • 2 Corinthians 10:5

Ephesians 3:20–21

> "Look at the birds. They don't plant or harvest or store food in barns, for your heavenly Father feeds them. And aren't you far more valuable to him than they are?"
>
> MATTHEW 6:26 NLT

CONTEXT

In this passage, Jesus was seated on a mountainside with his disciples around him. The crowds were large, and the people came from all over: Galilee, the Ten Towns, Jerusalem, all over Judea, and from the east of the Jordan River. Jesus taught them about many topics, which later collectively became known as the Sermon on the Mount.

MEANING

It's important to recognize that Jesus wasn't just talking to one people group, all of whom knew one another and had the same problems and experiences. The people in the crowds were from different towns and walks of life. We can only assume they were also from different social standings and levels of faith. Yet Jesus did not make exceptions as he taught. What he taught was, and still is, true for each individual person, regardless of gender, race, income level, or marital status. That means that his words are also true for us today.

The wonderful truth here is that God sees every little bird, including the one you see outside your window. And even more wonderful is that you are far more important to him than they are. In Matthew 6:26, Jesus explained to the crowd that no problem is too small for God. Jesus even asked the bold question, "Why worry at all?" Compared to the trials of human life, the needs of a bird are trivial. Jesus invites us to trust that our heavenly Father knows, sees, and is capable of providing for us.

APPLICATION

Focus today on God's love for you and his miraculous provision. Dare to believe that he cares for you that deeply—and not only for your physical needs, but for your emotional and relational needs as well.

So take your eyes off your circumstance and place them on God. Remember that he wants you to depend on him. He delights in taking care of your every need. While we can come up with a thousand reasons to worry, Jesus dares us to believe.

ADDITIONAL READING

Proverbs 3:5–6 • Psalm 23

> "Christ Jesus who died—
> more than that, who was raised
> to life—is at the right hand of God
> and is also interceding for us."
>
> ROMANS 8:34

CONTEXT

In this incredibly hopeful chapter of the Bible—Romans 8—
Paul delivers the jaw-dropping news that Christian believers
simply cannot be condemned. He reminds us that, because
we belong to Christ, we are showered with grace-filled blessings, including true freedom, privileges as children of God,
and assistance from the Spirit in our prayers. That last point
is where we'll focus today.

MEANING

Paul tells us that something mysterious happens when we
don't know what to pray. "Christ Jesus . . . is also interceding
for us."

Interceding is a fancy word for praying. And Paul thought
this sort of divine intercession was important enough that he
mentioned it not once but twice. A few verses earlier, Paul
writes, "The Spirit himself intercedes for us" (Romans 8:26).

Think about it: All three members of the Trinity are working on our behalf. The Spirit is praying for us (v. 26). Jesus is
praying for us (v. 34). And God is always listening.

The Triune God is assisting you in the work of prayer when you are tongue-tied and troubled.

APPLICATION

What is weighing on your heart today? Maybe the figures aren't adding up when you're paying the bills. Or, if you're a parent, maybe it feels like you're failing to really get through to the young people entrusted to your care. Maybe you're waiting for a diagnosis as you're reading these words today.

Life can be pretty overwhelming and anxiety-inducing, and sometimes it's hard to know how to pray and express our hearts fully and honestly.

Even if you can't find the right words to summon divine help, you are not left alone. God is with you, and he is in you. He joins you every day, in your everyday work and relationships, not only to equip you but to pray for you.

The Lord sees your clenched jaw, hears your sighs, and responds to your whispered plea, "Help me out here, Jesus, because I don't know what to do."

In his letter to the Romans, Paul says that Jesus not only listens, he is interceding for us!

Is it hard for you to believe that Jesus prays for us? How might you take one step today toward believing that is true for you?

Try this: Call out to Jesus and ask him to do the heavy lifting in prayer, to turn your worries into prayers, in accordance with his will.

ADDITIONAL READING

Romans 8:26 • Hebrews 7:25 • 1 John 2:1

> "I sought the LORD, and he
> answered me; he delivered
> me from all my fears."
>
> PSALM 34:4

Psalm 34 is both a wisdom psalm and a praise psalm. This was written in reference to David and his escape from Abimelech, the king of Gath from 1 Samuel 21.

It is believed that the king's personal name was actually Achish, and Abimelech was his throne name. Gath was a Philistine city and, based upon David's actions to try and escape from it, it was not a safe place for him to be.

David acted like he was mentally insane in order to flee because he could have died at the hands of this people. At this point in history, David was a fugitive, running from Saul and his army. It was through these years of trials and hardships that David learned to pray and trust in the Lord.

MEANING

Even in the most desperate situations or circumstances, we can choose to not fear because of the presence of the Lord surrounding us. David's praise unto the Lord is depicted in this verse, as he's proclaiming that God delivered him in response to his prayers. David specifically sought the Lord, Yahweh, and the Lord responded immediately, delivering David from his fears of death and the feelings that accompanied it.

APPLICATION

No matter what fears you are facing today, you can confidently cry out to the Lord, trusting that he hears and sees
you. You serve a God who reigns above all, and his deliverance of your fears may look different than you expected.
It could look like it did for David, and he learned to pray,
praise, and trust the Lord amidst his fears.

ADDITIONAL READING

Isaiah 12   •   Psalm 46   •   Psalm 91

Jonah 2   •   2 Timothy 1 (v. 7)

"But now, this is what the LORD says—
he who created you, Jacob,
he who formed you, Israel:
'Do not fear, for I have redeemed you;
I have summoned you by name;
you are mine.'"

ISAIAH 43:1

CONTEXT

In Isaiah 43, God speaks to his people, the Israelites, who are living in captivity on enemy soil. He encourages them— the day is coming when they will be set free and restored to their own land. He hasn't forgotten them and promises to be with them no matter what danger they may face.

MEANING

"I have summoned you by name." Here, God calls the Israelites, but he calls to us today too (see John 10:3). For God— who knows every mountain, star, and blade of grass—to call us by name, we must be precious to him. In fact, Isaiah 43:4 says, "You are precious and honored in my sight." When someone is precious to you, you care about every part of their life—even their worries.

Not only does God care about our worries, but he offers us peace in their place. When God says, "You are mine," it harkens to the Israelites' covenant with him. We who believe

in Jesus are also in a covenant with him (see Hebrews 8–9).
That means all that's ours is his, and all that's his is ours.
So he goes with us, even into the most troubled times and
places, and we are secure in his love (see Romans 8:38–39).
We can even ask him to exchange our worries for his peace
and confidence.

In this powerful verse, God reminds us that we're precious
to him and that he made us. Who else would know us more
intimately than the one who made us? He already knows our
anxious thoughts and isn't surprised by them. He loves for us
to ask for his help.

APPLICATION

Take a few minutes to consider what it means to be part of
God's family and to belong to him. Some benefits of belonging to a healthy family are shared resources, unconditional
love, and a safe place to talk about anything.

Because God is our safe place, we can bring all our worries and anxieties to him. Try setting aside a few minutes
every day to tell God about your worries. It may be difficult,
but imagine yourself physically handing your concerns over
to God and entrusting them to him (see 1 Peter 5:7). Then
watch how he takes care of you. He will bring resolution in
his perfect timing.

ADDITIONAL READING

Romans 8:31–39 • Psalm 100:3 • Isaiah 44:21

"I have told you these things, so that in me you may have peace. In this world you will have trouble. But take heart! I have overcome the world."

JOHN 16:33

CONTEXT

Jesus spoke these words to his disciples in the garden of Gethsemane, only hours before he would be betrayed, tried, and condemned to die by crucifixion. His disciples didn't know this was coming, and Jesus' prediction that they would soon be scattered and grieving seemed impossible after the joyful welcome they'd received coming into Jerusalem. Instead of ending with a warning, though, Jesus spoke words of hope, looking past the cross to his resurrection.

MEANING

It's a strange way to promise peace—Jesus starts by telling his disciples that they are about to go through a time of sorrow and fear. *How is that peaceful?* they might have wondered, especially after Good Friday, when their teacher was killed and it seemed like the world had won.

Still, Jesus' words, "Take heart!" are a command in the original language, not just an inspirational phrase but something God wanted them—and us—to actively do. It could be phrased "Choose hope!" or "Be encouraged!" When life is going well and we have a long list of blessings, that's easy enough to do. But some seasons, taking heart might be among the hardest of God's commandments to follow. Until we remember the rest of the verse: "I have overcome the world."

No matter how battle-weary we feel, God fights for us, and he's already won the war. Sin and Satan, death and hell were all beaten on the cross.

We can sometimes feel like the disciples huddled together in the dark after Jesus' death, wondering if all hope is lost—but that's when Jesus shows up to remind us that nothing can stop his conquering love.

APPLICATION

The trouble of this world will take many different forms during our life: conflict in our families and churches, physical or financial struggles, depression or natural disasters, or brokenness in the headlines and in our hearts. Whenever you're tempted to despair, remember Jesus' words. There isn't a single area of pain or problem we could ever experience that God has not overcome in the death and resurrection of Jesus. Because of this, we can expect troubles to come, but we can live joyfully in the midst of them.

ADDITIONAL READING

Psalm 27:14 • Jeremiah 1:19 • 2 Corinthians 4:8–9

> "But seek first his kingdom and his righteousness, and all these things will be given to you as well."
>
> MATTHEW 6:33

CONTEXT

Matthew, who wrote this Gospel, was a former tax collector who left his work to follow Jesus, becoming one of Christ's twelve apostles. Tax collecting was a despised profession by the Jewish people, as it was a way to get rich at the expense of your fellow countrymen. Matthew's account of Jesus' life places an emphasis on the fulfilling of Old Testament promises and prophecies.

MEANING

This verse is within the Sermon on the Mount—the longest continuous teaching of Jesus recorded in the Gospels. Jesus preached this sermon to his followers, and it covered everything from instructions on how to obey God to how to pray with humility to how to know who is a true follower of God. This verse is found within several paragraphs in the middle of the sermon, and it focuses on how to live a life free of worry.

Worry weighs us down and makes us forget that God takes care of us. We are told in this passage not to worry about food or clothes or what tomorrow will bring or even our very lives. God has these things under control. He takes care of

41

the birds of the air and the flowers of the field—surely he
can take care of you too!

So then, what are we supposed to be thinking about, if
not these things? God and his kingdom! These are eternal
things that will lift us up rather than drag us down. They are
worthy of our time and our hearts. And this verse goes on to
say that when we do focus on the things of God, he'll take
care of the things we need here on earth as well.

APPLICATION

It's ironic: If we focus on ourselves, we will be personally
miserable. But if we focus on God, not only will we honor
him, we'll also get all the things we need. And we'll have
peace of heart and mind thrown in for good measure!

This isn't easy, of course. We all worry about having our
needs met, and we worry about what the future holds. That's
why God reminds us again and again in Scripture to fight
this very human tendency, and to remind ourselves that God
is bigger than anything we face, and that he loves us and
cares about our needs.

Read through this passage today (Matthew 6:28–34).
Meditate on it. Consider memorizing it. It will serve you well
throughout your life.

ADDITIONAL READING

Psalm 34 • Psalm 4

> ## "You who fear the LORD, trust in the LORD! He is their help and their shield."
>
> **PSALM 115:11 ESV**

CONTEXT

Before verse 1 in Psalm 115, we see the line "To Your Name Give Glory." That's what this psalm is all about: giving glory to God! The psalmist discusses pagan gods—or idols—and reminds us that unlike those gods, our God works, speaks, listens, and feels. As such, he is the living God and is worthy of all glory.

MEANING

This verse has a clear command: "Trust in the LORD." Trusting in him requires more than simply telling him you trust him or thinking that you trust him. To trust in God, you have to submit to him. What are you trusting him with if you don't give your life and its circumstances over to him? It's easy to "trust" in God when you have control of your situation, but it's a lot harder when you let go and let him take the reins.

This verse also has a clear promise: "He is [your] help and [your] shield." When you fear the Lord and put your trust in him, he promises to be your help. You won't enter into a relationship with God that lacks follow-through. Your prayers will not fall on deaf ears. In contrast with the pagan gods who "have ears, but do not hear," God listens to all that you cry out, and he will be your help (Psalm 115:6). God will also be your shield, but you have to let him protect you. Be reminded of God's kindness in this verse. All you have to do is trust him and let him work.

APPLICATION

What is something that you're clinging on to and can submit to the Lord? Maybe it's something you're grieving or fearing. No matter what it is, it may be causing you to be anxious. Write down your worry in a notebook or on a scrap piece of paper. Circle it, and label that circle *God*. Pray that God will give you his help with your worries, that he will be your shield from pain and anxiety. Tell God your worry and give it over to him. Have peace in knowing his promise: to be your help and your shield.

ADDITIONAL READING

Psalm 46:1 • Colossians 3:2 • Matthew 11:28

> ## "Everyone who calls on the name of the Lord will be saved."
> ROMANS 10:13

CONTEXT

The book of Romans is a letter written by the apostle Paul to the Christians living in Rome. Scholars believe he wrote it from Corinth and had never visited Rome up to that point. The main reason for the letter was to give the new believers there a clear understanding of the basics of the Christian faith, the gospel, and the Christian's identity and responsibilities in Christ.

MEANING

This chapter of Romans begins with Paul sharing his heart for his own people—the Jews. This is a remarkable thing, considering how ruthlessly they've been persecuting him. Paul commends them for their zeal for God but says they don't know the true way to approach him. They believe it's through righteousness, but it is in fact through faith.

Paul paints a wonderful word picture to help his readers understand, saying that it isn't about us trying to "ascend to heaven" to bring Christ down. No, he's already here among us! This is a beautiful picture of God's grace. It's not our religious efforts or obedience that will bring us to God, but rather Christ's efforts and obedience.

So what, then, separates those who are in a relationship with God and those who aren't? Faith. The passage goes on to describe what this looks like. In a nutshell, the kind of faith that saves is the kind of faith that asks to be saved. Which brings us to our key verse: Everyone who calls on the name of the Lord will be saved. How much faith does it take to be saved? Just enough to ask the Lord. This is a promise for everyone. This is indeed good news.

APPLICATION

If you don't already have a relationship with God, call on Christ today! But calling on the name of the Lord is not only for salvation. We who are in God's family can continue to call on him for all our needs. As verse 12 of this chapter says, "the same Lord is Lord of all and richly blesses all who call on him." Continue calling on him daily and he will bless you richly.

ADDITIONAL READING

Isaiah 55:6–7 • Psalm 4

"Do not fear, for I am with you;
Do not be afraid, for I am your God.
I will strengthen you, I will also help
    you,
I will also uphold you with My
    righteous right hand."

ISAIAH 41:10 NASB

CONTEXT

The Israelites, God's people, are in exile because of their long history of willful sin against God and one another, and because they didn't heed his years of warnings to repent and avoid this painful consequence. And yet, he gives them this comforting message.

MEANING

In the immediate context, God was speaking to the Israelites, but he speaks to us today through this passage too. He tells us where we can find assurance when we are afraid: in his presence. Even when we are far from everything comfortable or normal, even when it seems we have every reason to fear, we can rest in his powerful presence, his strength, his tender love, his promise to uphold us.

And he always keeps his promises. Even when we, like the Israelites, are in a mess of our own making, he is with us. In the previous verse, he says, "I have chosen you and have

not rejected you" (Isaiah 41:9 NASB). He doesn't wait until we
have it all together. He reaches into our uncertainty, even our
sometimes-crippling anxiety, and steadies us, reminding us
that he's near, that he sees.

He shows how well he knows our tendencies when he says,
"Do not be afraid." Focusing on the unknown only adds to
our fears. Remembering God's goodness and meditating on
his character brings fresh perspective, peace, and courage.

He doesn't tell us not to be afraid because nothing bad
will ever happen; he tells us not to be afraid because he is
with us. Psalm 16:11 says, "In your presence is fullness of
joy." Joy isn't fleeting happiness. Joy holds on to hope in uncertainty because of a deep-seated assurance that God will
make all things right in the end (see Revelation 21:1–5).

How incredibly forgiving and merciful God is to give such
a message of hope to the Israelites in exile. How generous he
is to reach out to us even when we push him away.

APPLICATION

Take a few minutes to soak in the mystery of God's mercy
and love. Think back on how he has comforted and helped
you in times of anxiety.

Start keeping a record of those God moments. You can
refer back to this record daily or whenever you feel afraid, to
remind yourself of his love and nearness.

ADDITIONAL READING

Psalm 145:18 • Psalm 86:15 • Psalm 73:26 • 1 John 4:16

> "God is our refuge and strength,
> an ever-present help in trouble."
> PSALM 46:1

CONTEXT

The psalms are songs full of deep emotion and can serve as a helpful guide as we pour out our own fears, distress, and praise before God. Psalm 46 is near the beginning of book 2 of Psalms, which introduces the sons of Korah, and has many songs of lament and distress, but also has a firm reliance on God's faithfulness. There are many types of psalms; this particular one is a song of confidence in God's power and delivering hand.

MEANING

Psalm 46:1 sets up the idea that God is our refuge in times of trouble; the following verses expound on the "trouble." So then, when looking at this verse, it is important to also look at the two verses that follow:

"Therefore we will not fear, though the earth give way and the mountains fall into the heart of the sea, though its waters roar and foam and the mountains quake with their surging."

It does not say that God's help means bad things won't happen. On the contrary, these verses paint a vivid picture of a world full of upheaval and strife. In the Ancient Near East, the sea was considered a terrifying thing. It was unpredictable. It could kill you in an instant. So the image of the sea roaring and foaming and sucking even the mighty mountains into its depths must have been a very powerful image. And yet, the authors declare, "we will not fear." Why will we not fear? Because of verse 1: "God is our refuge and strength, an ever-present help in trouble."

Notice the psalm says, "God is . . . our strength." It is not we who are strong in the face of loss or fear, but God who is strong on our behalf. And he is not far away but "ever-present." He is our help. He is our safe place. He is our strength.

APPLICATION

Next time you feel yourself getting overwhelmed by anxiety, remember the truths of Psalm 46:1. Remind yourself that you don't need to fear, because God is right here with you. He is the only true shelter in a world thrown into chaos. He is your help in times of trouble.

As we saw before, the Psalms were written as songs where the authors poured out their hearts to God, and we can use them as guides for our own prayers. If you are having trouble clinging to the promise of Psalm 46:1, you can try praying it, with something like, "God, I am afraid. It feels like the earth is giving way beneath me. I know you said you are an ever-present help in trouble, so please help me now. Help me to take refuge in you. Help me to stop trying to be strong and trust in your strength instead. Help me to feel your presence near me through all this."

ADDITIONAL READING

Psalm 46:10 • Psalm 145:14 • Deuteronomy 31:6

> "For God has not given us a spirit
> of fear and timidity, but of power,
> love, and self-discipline."
>
> 2 TIMOTHY 1:7 NLT

CONTEXT

Second Timothy is a letter written from the apostle Paul to
Timothy. Paul knew Timothy well, as they traveled together
for a time during his second missionary journey. In the opening section of this letter, Paul is encouraging Timothy by reminding him of his family's strong legacy of faith.

MEANING

Verse 7 expands on this encouragement. Paul is telling Timothy to be bold! To fan into flames the spiritual gift that God
had given him. While we aren't told here what spiritual gift
Timothy was given, we can be led to believe that Timothy
may have been unsure or timid about it and was perhaps letting himself be ruled by fear.

Fear is a tool of the enemy that exists to keep us from
advancing the kingdom of God. It distracts us from trusting
him, and instead tempts us to protect ourselves and rely on
our own abilities. Fear very well could have been holding
Timothy back from preaching the Good News. But it is God
whom he needed to depend on, and it is God that we need
to depend on. Because while Satan may taunt us with fear of
looming dangers, God offers us power, unconditional love,

and the ability for cultivating a calm, well-balanced mind
(see the Amplified Bible translation).

APPLICATION

The devil loves it when we shrink back and hide because of
fear. And he continually whispers lies to keep us in docile
submission. But God is not in fear. We need to recognize the
things of God, rise up, and take hold of them! In those moments of fear, we need to think about what lies on the other
side of our faith. What kind of power might await us when
we take our thoughts captive and turn them to Christ? There
is no magic wand that makes fear disappear. Our enemy is
strong. But we have within ourselves, by the power of the
Holy Spirit, the ability to shut down our fears and claim
God's power.

When fears rise up, take them captive. Refuse to dwell on
them. Instead, dwell on the character of God. God is light,
and in him there is no darkness. He does not change like
shifting shadows. He shields all who take refuge in him and
is full of compassion. Practice this today and watch as his
power overtakes the fears of the enemy.

ADDITIONAL READING

1 John 1:5 • James 1:17 • Psalm 18:30 • Psalm 116:5

> ## "The LORD will fight for you,
> ## and you have only to be silent."
>
> EXODUS 14:14 ESV

CONTEXT

One of the five books of the law in the Bible, Exodus continues where Genesis leaves off. In this book, God frees the Israelites from four hundred years of forced labor in Egypt. The angel of the Lord then joins the Israelites on their journey to the Holy Land, which is led by Moses. During this time, God makes a covenant with his people and gives Moses the Ten Commandments while atop Mount Sinai.

MEANING

As the Egyptians pursue the Israelites in the wilderness, God tells Moses, "I will harden Pharaoh's heart," making the Israelites' fight for freedom even more challenging (Exodus 14:4). They begin questioning why Moses ever led them out of Egypt, and their anxiety heightens when they realize that Pharaoh is close. Surely, they must have had it better in Egypt, right?

Wrong. The Israelites have yet to understand the goodness of the Lord, because they are just coming to know him for the first time in over four hundred years. What they don't understand yet is that he has been with them all this time. He knows what they've experienced. He knows their sins. And yet, he loves them because they are his people. So while

Pharaoh may be getting close to the Israelites, God is closer and his plan for them is good.

What this means for you and me is that no matter what our circumstance, no matter how close our fears may be, the Lord and all his goodness is closer still. When we don't have the words because our worries are too loud, God will make much from our silence.

APPLICATION

It's hard to sit still and listen when anxiety is booming. Challenge yourself to find God's voice through all the noise. Let him reveal the ways he's been fighting for you, even if you think you've been fighting alone. With patience, you will see that God's fight for you reaches far and wide. His fight for you mimics his love for you; it is boundless, and it is forever. You don't have to ask God to battle on your behalf when you just can't find the words—he's already doing it.

As you start to see God's work in your day-to-day, you will soon realize that your battle is already won. This won't wash away the worry and is certainly not a quick fix, but it should encourage you to fall on God when you just need his rest.

ADDITIONAL READING

Genesis 28:16　•　Deuteronomy 31:8　•　Psalm 46:10

> "The temptations in your life are no different from what others experience. And God is faithful. He will not allow the temptation to be more than you can stand. When you are tempted, he will show you a way out so that you can endure."
>
> 1 CORINTHIANS 10:13 NLT

CONTEXT

First Corinthians is a letter the apostle Paul wrote to Christians in Corinth, a major port city in Greece. He wrote the letter to answer several questions posed by members of the Corinthian church. He also addressed the rampant immorality of the city, which had influenced the Corinthian church as well. The Corinthian Christians faced many temptations.

MEANING

In an attempt to comfort someone who's suffering, well-meaning Christians will often say that God does not give us more than we can handle, meaning God will give us problems and temptations, but he wouldn't give them to us if he knew that we weren't strong enough to handle them. But this is a misreading of the passage. James 1:13 says that God does not tempt anyone.

Take a close look and you'll see what 1 Corinthians 10:13 actually says: Many others experience the same kinds of temptations and struggles, but God will give us the strength we specifically need to face any trial or temptation that comes our way. He will be faithful no matter what we're going through, and he will see us through to the other side.

Notice also that Paul doesn't say that temptation is wrong. Temptation itself is not a sin. We know this because even Jesus was tempted by Satan (Matthew 4:1).

APPLICATION

Isn't it comforting to know that other people experience the same kinds of temptations and struggles you're experiencing? God hasn't singled you out to make you suffer simply because he thinks you're strong enough to handle it.

When you're tempted or when you're suffering, don't blame God. He is not tempting you, testing you, or sending trouble your way. Turn to him and ask for help. He'll be faithful to you, walk alongside you, and show you the way out.

ADDITIONAL READING

James 1:13 • Matthew 4:1 • John 16:33

"But they that wait upon the LORD shall renew their strength; they shall mount up with wings as eagles; they shall run, and not be weary; and they shall walk, and not faint."

ISAIAH 40:31 KJV

CONTEXT

While the book of Isaiah encompasses many themes, including God's holiness and judgment, the overarching message of this major prophet is salvation—fitting, since Isaiah means "the salvation of the Lord" and the book contains perhaps the clearest Old Testament articulations of the gospel. After prediction of the Babylonian exile in Isaiah 39, chapter 40 shifts to an emphasis on comforting Israel and providing the hope and encouragement people will need through the coming dark times.

MEANING

In verse 31, the beautiful promise of the Lord's sufficiency, of his ability and willingness to be the inexhaustible source of their strength, is made to those who rely on him. People who wait for him will make it to the end. They will run but not tire, equipped to keep up the pace indefinitely; they will continue walking as long as required and will not be overcome by circumstances.

The choice of the eagle to illustrate is particularly apt because to complete any endurance challenge, unflagging strength—not speed or showmanship—is what's needed. So while there are birds that fly faster and soar higher than eagles, no other bird of prey is stronger or more powerful than certain eagle species, which have unmatched wing strength.

APPLICATION

As we go through life, whether in a smooth patch or a rough one, it can be tempting to try to make our own way, to handle things ourselves and expect God to bless these self-directed efforts. But that approach is contrary to his instructions. We are to trust in God and his ways, not devise our own solutions with our limited perspective and finite resources.

When we trust the Lord and wait on him, seek him in prayer, and search his Word, allowing him to move in our circumstances instead of trying to wrest control, we are supplied with his sustaining strength. If, however, we act as the youth and young men in the preceding verse 30, we can expect to grow weary and faint, to utterly fail. Why? Because we are trusting in our own strength and abilities, which ultimately prove insufficient.

It isn't always easy to wait, but if we can discipline ourselves to do so, we will soar, knowing that it is the Lord who keeps us aloft.

ADDITIONAL READING

John 15:5 • Isaiah 40:28 • Psalm 27:1

Proverbs 3:5–6 • Galatians 6:9

"Lord, my every desire is in front
    of you;
my sighing is not hidden from you."

PSALM 38:9 CSB

CONTEXT

This psalm is credited to David, the shepherd-turned-king of
Israel whose story and writings are so prevalent in the Bible.
It's unclear at what point in David's life he wrote this psalm,
in which he confesses the "foolishness" of an unnamed sin,
and even states, "I am anxious because of my sin" (38:18 CSB).
Fearing God will abandon him, David pleads with God to
stay near and help him in his time of need.

MEANING

It is thought that David composed about half of the psalms.
Read just a few of these songs and you can't miss the depth
of his emotions to and about God. Throughout Psalm 38,
David expresses the torment he feels because of his sin, and
asks God not to punish him in anger (v. 1). "My insides are
full of burning pain . . ." he writes, "[and] I am faint and se-
verely crushed" (vv. 7–8).

And yet, despite David's anguish and fear, he knows God's
power and love:

> "Lord, my every desire is in front of you;
> my sighing is not hidden from you" (Psalm 38:9 CSB).

What a remarkable example for all of us. No matter the circumstances of our anguish—self-inflicted or not—God knows what we're going through. He knows our healthy and unhealthy desires. And if we can't or won't call out to God, he hears even our sighs.

A bit later in the psalm, David describes loved ones, including friends and relatives, standing back from his affliction (v. 11). That can happen to us too. Sometimes people aren't sure how to best help a person who is struggling. We can't forget, though, that God loves us and cares about what we're going through.

APPLICATION

Although God can hear our sighs, we shouldn't hold back about expressing deep emotions to him. Talk to him, sing to him, journal prayers to him. Share what's on your heart. Praise him for his love and faithfulness. Thank him for how he's provided for you. And when times are tough, let him know how you feel. After all, more than forty of the 150 psalms are considered psalms of lament, expressing grief or sorrow.

You may also find comfort by reading through the book of Psalms and making certain ones your own prayers or songs. It's strangely reassuring that what we go through today is not very different from when David and other writers of Psalms lived. And the God they trusted is the same God we can trust.

ADDITIONAL READING

Psalm 10:17 • Matthew 6:8 • Romans 8:26–27

> "Have I not commanded you?
> Be strong and courageous! Do
> not be terrified nor dismayed,
> for the LORD your God is with
> you wherever you go."
>
> JOSHUA 1:9 NASB

CONTEXT

After forty years of wandering in the wilderness, the people of Israel were all abuzz—God was finally leading them into the land he had promised them. But it wouldn't be easy. Israel's enemies still occupied kingdoms and cities inside the promised land, and they weren't leaving without a fight. This book follows Israel and their leader, Joshua, as they trust God and come into their inheritance.

MEANING

After Moses' passing, God chose Joshua to finally lead the Israelites into the land he had promised them decades before. Joshua had seen God perform countless miracles in his life: parting the Red Sea, providing food from heaven, and even manifesting himself as pillars of cloud and fire to lead the Israelites. Even with his decades of military experience, Joshua still needed encouragement from God and others to continue walking in faith.

The phrase "be strong and courageous" appears five times in the book of Joshua: four instances directed to Joshua in chapter 1—three of them by God—and one to the Israelites. In every instance, this command to "be strong and courageous" is surrounded by promises, reminders, and warnings.

In verse 6, God commands Joshua to "be strong and courageous" because God is going to fulfill his promise. Joshua is not going to go out onto the battlefield without God's strength and favor, and God is going to give the Israelites victory in conquering the promised land because he never reneges on his promises.

In verses 7 and 8, God connects being strong and courageous to faithfully following his Word. Not believing in God's Word nor taking it seriously had been the sin that forced the Israelites to wander in the wilderness for forty years. But if Joshua follows God's commands, rules, and promises, he will "have success wherever [he goes]." By contrast, the Israelites are warned that whoever doesn't obey Joshua's commands from God will be put to death (v. 18). Joshua is encouraged to follow God boldly, knowing God will fulfill his promises and the Israelites will faithfully follow.

As a punch of a conclusion, God leaves Joshua with verse 9—a clear command to move in strength, live courageously, and believe above all else that "the Lord [his] God is with [him] wherever [he goes]."

APPLICATION

Like Joshua, God has called his people to follow him into the unknown. A new job or home, dating and marriage, facing past traumas and sins—sometimes what God calls us to seems too big, too impossible. We begin to fear, question, drag our feet, or even walk away entirely, thinking we must not have heard him correctly.

God is not in the coddling business. He calls us from the shallow, calm waters of life into the deep end, because it's only out of our depth that we must trust and rely on him completely. It's there, in the deep and the wild, that God fulfills his promises, our faith flourishes, and we grow closer to him.

This call to "be strong and courageous . . . not tremble or be dismayed" isn't a flippant encouragement; it's God's command. However our hearts may hurt or our knees wobble, we are commanded to move forward boldly and trustfully, one step at a time. Why? Because "the LORD your God is with you wherever you go." And God fulfills his promises.

ADDITIONAL READING

Deuteronomy 3:22 • Lamentations 3:57 • 1 Peter 3:14
Luke 12:7 • Isaiah 41:10

> "You came near when I called you,
> and you said, 'Do not fear.'"
>
> LAMENTATIONS 3:57

CONTEXT

Lamentations is a book of sadness, written after the fall of Jerusalem. Just before this verse, the author talks about feeling overwhelmed and unseen, just like the people of Israel. For a long time, they didn't listen to the warnings of the prophets to stop sinning, and they turned to other nations' wealth and status for comfort instead of crying out to God. With nowhere left to turn, many finally did call out for God's help, and this verse shows how God answered them.

MEANING

We all have different first reactions to a crisis like a job loss, the critical diagnosis of a loved one, or a stressful relationship. Some go into "planner mode" and try to create a practical solution. Others find a friend to cry with or ask for advice. Many try to be prepared by spending time thinking through the worst-case scenarios of what could come next.

These responses aren't necessarily bad, but none are the ultimate solution to the fear that threatens to overwhelm our hearts in hard times. Like the author of this passage, we need to call out for God to be near to us. Instead of waiting until we have no options left, we should start by coming to God first.

His response will always be, "Do not fear." Not condemning us for being afraid, but telling us there's no need for it. He is holding on to us tightly, a good Father whose perfect love casts out fear . . . if we just ask.

APPLICATION

What does it look like for you to call on the name of the Lord in hard times? One way might be to look up a list of the names and titles God uses for himself in the Bible, such as Savior, Good Shepherd, Counselor, and Defender. As you read through the list, think about what each of those names means for you and your life situation.

For example, as your Savior, God can forgive your sins or help you forgive someone who has wronged you. As the Good Shepherd, you can trust him to lead you and protect you from harm. As you pray through the names of God, reflect on the ones that stand out most to you in the season you're in. Remember them in moments you're tempted to fear, and you'll be able to stand firm in the truth of who God is and what he does for his children.

ADDITIONAL READING

Genesis 16:13 • Psalm 33:18 • 1 John 4:18

> "May the God of hope fill you with all joy and peace as you trust in him, so that you may overflow with hope by the power of the Holy Spirit."
>
> ROMANS 15:13

CONTEXT

In this section of Paul's letters to the Romans, we are told that Christ came not only to set the Jews free, but also that his salvation extends to the Gentiles. There is no one on earth whom Christ cannot save when salvation is God's will and when we believe in Jesus wholeheartedly. Paul reminds us that there is great hope in God's mercy.

MEANING

By his death on the cross, Jesus gave hope to those who believe in him. The word *hope* is probably part of your daily vocabulary: "I hope you have a good day," or, "I hope you feel better soon." We love to hope for one another and even for ourselves. But biblical hope—the kind of hope we have from Jesus—is much deeper than the word we often say in passing.

For centuries, God's people had prophesied the coming of the Messiah. Paul actually shares some of those words in Romans 15. He quotes a few verses, including 2 Samuel 22:50 and Psalm 18:49: "Therefore I will praise you, LORD, among the nations; I will sing the praises of your name." God's people knew that the Messiah was going to come and that he would not only set them free but that he would set the nations free. This is God's promise. Our confidence in that promise, in the death and resurrection of Christ Jesus and all that it fulfilled, is hope.

When we have hope—that confidence in God's promise—we are filled with the Holy Spirit. He brings us joy and peace because we believe in Jesus. We believe that Jesus fulfilled the law. We believe that his death, his sacrifice, satisfied the great depth of our sin. In Jesus, you have hope; with hope, you have the Holy Spirit; and with the Holy Spirit, you have joy and peace.

APPLICATION

What is it that you're hoping for right now? Maybe you're hoping that your financial stress will be lessened this week or that you'll have an extra hour added to your day so that you can finish a project. Whatever it is you're hoping for, pray and ask God how he has already satisfied that hope through his Son. For the rest of the week, let biblical hope replace the worries you're facing.

ADDITIONAL READING

1 Peter 1:13 • Ephesians 1:18 • Hebrews 10:23

> "Therefore confess your sins
> to each other and pray for each
> other so that you may be healed.
> The prayer of a righteous person
> is powerful and effective."
>
> JAMES 5:16

CONTEXT

The book of James is a call to action for believers to ensure their faith is authentic and to produce word and deed accordingly. James 1:22 says believers shouldn't just listen to the Word, but that we should do what it says. The first chapter begins the call by addressing our reaction to trials and our response to hearing the Word of God.

MEANING

The book of James is a practical book, filled with wisdom for everyday living. The fifth chapter begins with a warning to rich oppressors that God is watching and will turn things against them. This flows into a call for patience that justice will be done.

From there, James goes on to talk about the effectiveness of prayer, specifically when it comes to healing. He tells his believers to call the elders to pray and anoint the sick with oil. But then the passage takes a surprising turn: Healing is linked to confession. Why is that?

So many things in our lives have a spiritual component that we sometimes ignore. There is a spiritual aspect to our relationships, our jobs, and our health. If we ignore the importance of confession and repentance, we might be missing out on the healing God wants for us. Being righteous—i.e., having our sins forgiven—makes a difference.

And the great news is, we don't have to pray alone. God asks us to pray in community, and have other righteous people pray over us as well. And he promises that these prayers have a great effect—they matter and have a great power. There is hope that comes in prayer, and not just our own prayers, but the prayers of our Christian brothers and sisters.

APPLICATION

If you're sick, have you considered asking your elders to pray over you? Maybe consider using oil as well, to anoint you as they call upon God for your healing. This sounds old-fashioned and maybe even weird to our modern ears, but God's Word is filled with wisdom that surpasses our own cultural norms of today.

ADDITIONAL READING

Mark 11:24 • Ephesians 6:18 • 1 John 5:14–15

> "Be strong and courageous.
> Do not be afraid or terrified
> because of them, for the LORD your
> God goes with you; he will never
> leave you nor forsake you."
>
> DEUTERONOMY 31:6

CONTEXT

Deuteronomy is a recording of speeches Moses gave to the Israelites as they prepared to enter Canaan. At the same time, it's also Moses' last words of instruction before his death and the transition of leadership to Joshua. In Deuteronomy, Moses emphasizes the key laws they will need to obey to honor God, emphasizing the battle that will be waged in their hearts to choose to obey the Lord rather than succumb to their own evil desires and the temptations that come from the nations around them.

MEANING

Moses was not allowed to go into the promised land himself, so he's nearing the time when he will no longer be able to lead them. He loves his people and wants to encourage them for the mighty tasks they are facing. But he also loves God and knows God is the only one who can enable them to succeed.

Here, Moses is like a coach pumping up his team before the last quarter of the big game. They've come this far and it hasn't been easy, but there's still more to do. The battle is real, but God is on their side, so victory is secure. "I will never leave you nor forsake you" has to be one of the most encouraging verses in the Bible. In fact, the author of Hebrews quotes it to encourage new believers to keep following the Lord.

The idea that God would never leave nor forsake the Israelites (and his followers today) is profound. Think of all the ways the Israelites fell short of God's will—through idolatry, sexual immorality, and ingratitude—and yet God still makes this promise. And they can be strong and take courage because they know God always keeps his promises.

APPLICATION

Similar to the Israelites, we fall short of God's perfect will as well, sinning daily through our actions and attitudes. But God forgives. His promises remain secure. When we are sealed in Christ, nothing can separate us from his love.

Cling to this promise and take courage. Whatever you're facing, God knows and is able to conquer. Be strong in him, knowing he is always by your side. Once you've called upon Christ's name as your Savior, you are his forever, an heir of God prepared to someday enter your own promised land.

Write this verse down and put it in your wallet or purse, and when you're feeling weak or discouraged, pull it out and read it to yourself. God's promises never fail.

ADDITIONAL READING

Hebrews 13 • Joshua 1 • Matthew 28:20

> "Anxiety weighs down the heart,
> but a kind word cheers it up."
>
> PROVERBS 12:25

CONTEXT

The book of Proverbs tells us directly in the first few verses what its purpose is: "For gaining wisdom and instruction." Chapters 10–22 are loosely grouped proverbs of King Solomon on a whole variety of subjects. What binds them together is less a logical argument or even a theme, and more the fact that, together, they give general principles that make for a healthy, whole life for someone who loves God. All of them teach very practical truth about how to live day to day.

MEANING

Life can feel heavy sometimes, can't it? Most of us expect to feel exhausted and weary when we're battling a physical challenge like a chronic illness or recovery from an injury, but sometimes we don't anticipate the toll things like stress, uncertainty, and fear have on us. Describing anxiety as weighing down the heart makes it the emotional equivalent of waking up with a barbell slung over your chest and carrying it around the rest of the day.

Proverbs is a realistic book, not just about what we do and say, but also about how we feel. The amount of time devoted to our emotions in the Bible tells us that God cares about all of us, including our hearts. And our hearts are often anxious.

Instead of just describing our natural state of worrying and fretting, though, Solomon provides a solution in this passage.

Feeling anxious? A kind word will lift some of that weight away. So surround yourself with people who encourage you, instead of pushing them away. Reread a letter or email that reminded you of something deeply true. Listen to music with lyrics that strengthen your heart. Go to familiar, underlined promises in the Bible and soak in those beautiful words.

And don't forget about the cheering power of giving a kind word to others too. Sometimes, what we really need to fight anxiety is to get our eyes off our own problems and serve others. We have an example of this in Jesus, who over and over again loved and served those around him. After his cousin, John the Baptist, died, Jesus went to be by himself with his disciples to pray and mourn . . . but crowds of people followed him. Instead of turning inward, he "had compassion on them" and taught them, later providing a miraculous meal (Mark 6:34). He could have joy through serving others, even on difficult days.

APPLICATION

Is there anyone in your life who might need a kind word today? Reach out to them, telling them you're praying for them or that you're thankful for the role they have in your life. Remember that in doing so, you're walking in Jesus' steps. And if you're in need of a kind word, reflect on what God says about you in Scripture. He is your heavenly Father, and you are his child. What could be more cheering than that?

ADDITIONAL READING

Ephesians 4:32 • Mark 6:31–34 • Proverbs 11:17

> ## "When I am afraid,
> ## I put my trust in you."
> PSALM 56:3 ESV

CONTEXT

The heading that accompanies Psalm 56 includes this line about the circumstances that inspired David to write it: "When the Philistines seized him in Gath." The account in 1 Samuel 21:10–15 describes David's actions as he fled from King Saul and went to Achish, the king of Gath, ultimately feeling such great fear there that he pretended to be insane in order to escape.

The verse that immediately follows, verse 4 of Psalm 56, begins, "In God, whose word I praise, in God I trust; I shall not be afraid."

MEANING

In the psalms we have a beautifully rich collection of poetry and songs. Many were written by David in response to the challenges he faced and in recognition of God's faithfulness in the midst of them. In this verse, and throughout the psalms, the realities of fear and danger are not dismissed. Instead, they are acknowledged, and from that humble honesty, David directs his own heart, and ours, to turn to God in trust.

Just before the account in 1 Samuel referenced above, David accepts from a priest the sword of Goliath, a tangible reminder of the victory God brought earlier in his life, when so many others were afraid. Yet here again he finds himself facing fear, beginning this verse with "When I am afraid," not *if.*

It is what he does with that fear that can guide and encourage us today. Let's see those lines from Psalm 56:3–4 (ESV) paired together here:

> "When I am afraid,
> I put my trust in you.
> In God, whose word I praise,
> in God I trust; I shall not be afraid."

APPLICATION

Consider memorizing these lines. Their rhythm and structure give us help for the times when we find ourselves feeling afraid. Like David, we can acknowledge our fear. We can turn our hearts and minds to placing our trust in God. We can praise him and his Word, perhaps even like David finding a creative outlet to express our worship. And in so doing, as we grow in trusting the God we praise, we shall not be afraid. And when we find ourselves having come through a victory and yet facing fear again, we can follow David's example and turn anew to the God we trust.

ADDITIONAL READING

1 Samuel 17:24, 45–51 • 1 Samuel 21:8–15 • Psalm 28:7

"When you pass through the waters,
I will be with you;
and when you pass through the
	rivers,
they will not sweep over you.
When you walk through the fire,
you will not be burned;
the flames will not set you ablaze."

ISAIAH 43:2

CONTEXT

This chapter of Isaiah focuses on God's love for and redemption of his people; it looks ahead to the deliverance of the Israelites from Babylon and, further, to the coming Redeemer of all believers. The early verses emphasize that God's people can take comfort and live fearlessly even in times of great trouble, knowing that their Creator and Savior is with them.

MEANING

Isaiah is both foretelling and retelling in this verse—a powerful combination for stirring up faith and confidence. With the same words the prophet is using to assure God's people they can trust the Lord to see them through all their current and future troubles, he is also reminding them of past occasions when God miraculously proved his ability

and faithfulness in delivering them: first when he parted the
Red Sea, allowing the Israelites to cross on dry land (to "pass
through the waters"), and again when he stopped the flow
of the flooded Jordan so the people could "pass through the
rivers."

In a more general reading of the verse, the elements of
water and fire signify all manner of danger, trouble, and
calamity that can befall people. This verse assures believers that A) they will not face trials alone; B) they will not be
overcome by or destroyed by the trouble or circumstances in
which they find themselves; and C) with God as their cham-
pion, they won't even be harmed—in essence, they will come
out unscathed, as proves to be the case for Shadrach, Me-
shach, and Abednego in the fiery furnace of Daniel 3. (Did
those three draw strength and courage from this very verse?)

APPLICATION

There is no doubt that in this life we will encounter difficulties; Jesus himself tells us so. Since we know the question is
not *if* we will have struggles but rather *when*—a word used
three times in this verse—our answer really must focus on
how we will weather our storms. In light of the awesome,
unequivocal promises of God's presence in and protection
through whatever troubles come our way, our *how* should
be characterized by faith, fearlessness, and peace because
God has assured us that we are not alone, that we will pass
through, we will walk through, and we will emerge—whole.

ADDITIONAL READING

Joshua 1:5–7 • Isaiah 41:10 • John 16:33 • Romans 8:31

> "You intended to harm me, but God intended it all for good. He brought me to this position so I could save the lives of many people."
>
> GENESIS 50:20 NLT

CONTEXT

These words were said by Joseph after returning from Canaan to bury his father, Jacob. His brothers were terrified that, now that their father was dead, Joseph would finally use his authority to seek revenge on them for leaving him for dead when he was young. Joseph surprises them by saying, "Don't be afraid of me. Am I God, that I can punish you?" (Genesis 50:19 NLT). He kindly promises to continue to care for his brothers and their families.

MEANING

There are very few people in the Bible who are spoken as highly of as Joseph. He endured some of the most difficult circumstances and betrayals and still honored the Lord in the midst of them. He refused to see his journey as one setback after another, but instead chose to have faith to believe that God was writing a much bigger story. There was a very long time between when Joseph had a dream as a teenager and when he was appointed over Pharaoh's kingdom as an adult. During that time there were some setbacks that seemed like they could have been the end of his story. For most of us, our circumstance informs our confidence, which then determines the measure of our faith. This is where Joseph took God at his word. He beautifully exemplified what it looks like to have your faith inform your confidence, regardless of the circumstance.

APPLICATION

Reading through Joseph's story, we should take note of a couple of things. First, Joseph was determined to walk in integrity no matter what life threw at him. And second, whether power was given or stripped away, he continued to use his gifts to glorify the Lord. I encourage you, next time you feel unsure about the future, set your sights on God's faithfulness. Remember that he is writing a book with your life that is bigger than the current chapter. Take him at his word. Allow your confidence to be informed by your faith, not your circumstance. Walk in integrity and continue to use your gifts to glorify God. Remember, this chapter is critical to the greater story, and there are more chapters that are yet to be written.

ADDITIONAL READING

Romans 8:28 • Philippians 1:6 • Jeremiah 29:11

> "When anxiety was great within me,
> your consolation brought me joy."
>
> PSALM 94:19

CONTEXT

The psalms are songs full of deep emotion and can serve as a helpful guide as we pour out our own fears, distress, and praise before God. The theme of Psalm 94 is how wickedness thrives on earth but God is still in control and will be victorious.

MEANING

We've all had times when our anxiety was great within us. Sometimes the cause of our anxiety is outward, such as a health scare, financial distress, or relational struggles. At other times we don't even know the cause of our anxiety—we just feel unsettled and scared and end up wondering what's wrong with us.

Regardless of the cause of your anxiety, there is an enemy at work that God must overcome. There are three enemies we have to deal with as Christians: the world, the devil, and ourselves. Sometimes the world fights against us through circumstances and antagonism from individuals or the culture around us. Sometimes the devil and his demons are antagonizing us because they hate God's people. At other times we wrestle with what's in ourselves—we give in to our sin nature and fallenness.

But in all these cases, just as this psalm says, God is our fortress. He is stronger than anything we could ever face.

Today's verse says God's consolation brings me joy. What are God's consolations? Other translations use the word *comforts*. God comforts us when we're facing trials, and we find joy in the reassurance that he's there and has our back. God is our refuge in all circumstances, and his love is "unfailing."

APPLICATION

Name your enemy. Sometimes we forget that we even have enemies, assuming that we just have bad luck. But your enemies are real, and it is helpful to know who/what they are so you can arm yourself and pray against them. But the good news is, regardless of your enemy, God is always stronger.

ADDITIONAL READING

Ephesians 6:10–18 • Psalm 46:1–3

> "Here I am! I stand at the door and knock. If anyone hears my voice and opens the door, I will come in and eat with that person, and they with me."
>
> REVELATION 3:20

CONTEXT

At St. Paul's Cathedral in London, you'll find the most well-traveled piece of artwork in history: William Holman-Hunt's oil painting *The Light of the World*. It is a powerful image, Christ standing in front of a curved wooden door at dusk, as if he's been on a long journey, as if he is looking for a place to rest. He knocks softly, calling our names in a gentlemanly way. Though Christ bears his own light, you can feel the coolness of the evening descending and the shadows creeping in. So, warm and comfortable in our homes, we should let Christ in, doing what would help him, giving him what he so desires—communion with us.

MEANING

Yet by doing so, we forget the larger context of Christ's words. In this section of Scripture, he is speaking to the Laodicean church, which has prided itself on being capable, self-sufficient, and accomplished. But in truth, they have become lukewarm in walking out their faith, wealth blinding them to their own poverty in spirit. He even threatens to spit them out (v. 16) in response.

APPLICATION

When life is going well, it is so easy to trust in our comforts, in our ability to mark off the to-do lists and control our schedules. The stable rhythms of life lull us into contentment. It becomes easier to have our commitments discipline us, rather than us set our own priorities. As Brian Houston of Hillsong has said, we are what we allow. Too often when crisis comes and worry rises up, what we have allowed into our lives crumbles under the pressure and us along with it.

If we look at Hunt's painting, he actually offers viewers these cautions as well—for a closer look shows the door is overgrown and lacks a handle. Living our lives, tending to other things, the door to our hearts has fallen out of use, and we haven't given Christ free rein to enter as he chooses. Fortunately, we see in this letter Christ issuing in one hand a sharp warning to keep faith as our bedrock, and in the other, deep grace. For even if we haven't opened the door recently, Christ still knows the way to us. In fact, he is already present, calling out, "Here I am!" For his claim that he stands at the door knocking comes not as one needing something from us, but instead as one who has braved the darkness to bring his light into our most secret places. For when the door is opened, no matter that there is chaos, that the money jar is empty, the child is absent, that one lies sick, he can mend all those things. His communion is always to our betterment.

ADDITIONAL READING

John 1:12 • Matthew 11:28–30 • Revelation 22:17

> "God, the Lord, is my strength;
> he makes my feet like the deer's;
> he makes me tread on my high places."
>
> HABAKKUK 3:19 ESV

CONTEXT

The prophet Habakkuk laments to God on behalf of the people of Judah, the Southern Kingdom of Israel. This book was written before the people of Judah were exiled into the land of Babylon, but were still in the midst of God's judgment on his people. In chapter 3, Habakkuk prays, recalling the goodness of the Lord and reminding us that our hope is in him.

MEANING

At the time that Habakkuk is writing, Judah is feeling the weight of God's judgment yet is still turning toward false gods and enemy nations for security and protection. The people of Judah actually blame Yahweh for their troubles. They are failing to recognize the mercy and grace of the Lord in their times of hardship. But in fact, even God's judgment on Judah is merciful! He cares for his people and, despite their sin, he still promises to fulfill the covenant made with their fathers.

Habakkuk, after some lamenting and a vision from the Lord, recognizes God's righteousness in the land and prays that God will be made known mighty. Our strength indeed comes from the Lord; he alone gives us assurance. Like a deer, stable-footed on a rocky slope, the Lord helps us face and overcome our challenges and weaknesses with confidence.

Even in the midst of our hardships, our worries, our anxieties, we may have joy in Christ Jesus. It is those very trials that sanctify our souls, making us each more like Christ. While it may be difficult to understand in the moment, these low places can bring us closer to God if we submit to him and believe that his goodness, mercy, love, grace, and joy will prevail above all else.

APPLICATION

Sometimes it feels like the walls around us are breaking down and crumbling inward. We do everything in our power to find stability. However, as Christians, we must acknowledge that we cannot have that stability without reliance on the Lord.

If you're able, take a prayer walk sometime today. Like Habakkuk, lament to the Lord; tell him your fears and frustrations. And like Habakkuk, praise God for his might, and remember that he alone is your strength. Just like your sure-footedness as you walk, the Lord goes before you in all things.

ADDITIONAL READING

Psalm 23:4 • James 1:2 • Romans 8:18

> "In peace I will lie down and sleep,
> for you alone, LORD,
> make me dwell in safety."
>
> PSALM 4:8

CONTEXT

The psalms are a collection of prayers and hymns written by David, Solomon, and several other ancient Israelites. Each and every psalm was inspired by God and serves to teach us and connect us to him in a deeper way. Psalm 4, written by David, is a prayer of distress, but ends in God's comfort and peace.

MEANING

This psalm begins with David crying out to God: "Answer me when I call to you" and "give me relief from my distress." Within this opening prayer, he goes on to acknowledge God's righteousness and his faithfulness to his followers. He also reminds God (and himself) that God has heard him before; it's in God's nature to listen to his people.

But from there the psalm takes an interesting turn: It moves from prayer to instruction. He tells his audience to be righteous, search their hearts, and refuse to sin. It is a reminder that God is holy—he's not just a genie we can call upon when we need something.

Then, shifting back into prayer mode, he asks God to shine his face upon us and fill us with joy. And after all that, he ends on the wonderful note of peace in the verse at the top of this page. It is knowing that the Lord is with us, protecting us, that allows us to lie down and sleep peacefully.

APPLICATION

One of the wonderful things about the psalms is that, for the most part, they're easy to understand. We can relate to the emotions, the desires, the cries of the heart. Such prayers cross any cultural or historical barriers.

Most of this psalm is a prayer, so pray it! Go through the words verse by verse, calling out to God and praising him for his goodness. In particular, pray this psalm before bedtime if you're struggling to sleep, reminding yourself that God has you in his hand and that he wants you to rest peacefully.

ADDITIONAL READING

Psalm 127 • 1 Samuel 23:14 • Mark 4:38–40

> "When Jesus had tasted it, he said,
> 'It is finished!' Then he bowed his
> head and gave up his spirit."
>
> JOHN 19:30 NLT

CONTEXT

In this passage of the Gospel of John, we are shown that
Jesus knew every single prophecy was complete.

MEANING

The word *finished* here is the Greek word *teleō*, which means
to pay (in full) or to fulfill or complete a command given. The
root word *telos* means to set out for a definite goal; it also
translates to *uttermost*. So we are looking at the final words
of Christ fulfilling what he promised to us, to the uttermost.

What did he promise?

John 3:16 (NLT) says, "For this is how God loved the world:
He gave his one and only Son, so that everyone who believes
in him will not perish but have eternal life."

In Isaiah 53:5 (NLT), the payment of Christ was prophesied, "But he was pierced for our rebellion, crushed for our
sins. He was beaten so we could be whole. He was whipped
so we could be healed."

John 10:10 (NASB): "The thief comes only to steal and kill
and destroy; I came so that they would have life, and have it
abundantly."

Through Scripture we can see that we are promised eternal life, full payment of our sins, complete healing and an abundant life in the here and now.

Jesus paid for everything on the cross, so when he said, "It is finished," he meant that everything that could possibly be paid for was paid for and done for us; now we only need to receive. That abundant life described in John 10:10 is waiting for us; the Passion Translation says it this way: "But I have come to give you everything in abundance, more than you expect—life in its fullness until you overflow!"

APPLICATION

We are meant to be overflowing in the fullness of life! Jesus paid for us to live free from the weights of sin, fear, doubt, worry, and so much more. We have fullness waiting for us as we simply receive.

In the middle of the storms of life it can be difficult to be still and listen for the voice of our loving heavenly Father, but I encourage you to sit back, take a deep breath, and hear the word of our Lord say to you, "My child, it is finished."

ADDITIONAL READING

Isaiah 53 • Psalm 27

> "You will keep in perfect peace
> those whose minds are steadfast,
> because they trust in you."
>
> ISAIAH 26:3

CONTEXT

The book of Isaiah was written by the prophet Isaiah, who served as a messenger to the people of the Southern Kingdom of Judah for more than fifty years (around 740 to 686 BC). His calling was to point out the sin that ran rampant amongst the people of Judah at this time, and he often spoke God's words directly to the four kings who reigned during his ministry. He accomplished his calling both by preaching the truth of Judah's present circumstances and by prophesying about their future, covering everything from impending national judgment to the coming of Christ to the hope of a new heaven and a new earth.

MEANING

One of the major themes in Isaiah is that as God's people obey his will by trusting in him, they will find peace and prosperity in their lives. This didn't mean the people would never experience hardship or disharmony; in fact, they were experiencing much of both. However, a prevalent sin amongst the people of Judah during this time was building up wealth by exploiting the poor and marginalized people. God saw the people were not trusting him to take care of them and were attempting to find peace and security on their own, even if it meant taking cruel advantage of others who were already at risk in their community.

The original Hebrew does not contain the word for *perfect* prior to *peace* but instead actually repeats itself by saying "peace, peace." God and his inspired writers always use repetition in the Bible with specific intention, and here, this repetition is interpreted to mean real, true, constant, and lasting peace.

The people of Judah did not live in a peaceful time, so they were tempted not to remain steadfast in their knowledge of whom God had proven himself to be and what he had promised them. Isaiah is reminding them that their sinful attempts to find peace through other means will never lead to the perfect peace God can give them.

APPLICATION

Like the people of Judah, we all go through times where peace feels hard to find. Sometimes you may try to control your external or internal, temporary or permanent peace by taking matters into your own hands, running away from unpeaceful situations, or getting caught in mental patterns of worry and anxiety. God wants you to know that, while worldly peace may indeed be hard to find, his perfect peace is always available to you.

When you steadfastly set your mind on him, day to day and moment by moment, and trust in him more than anything else, he will not only give you the peace you seek; he has the power to keep you in a state of true peace no matter what happens.

ADDITIONAL READING

Proverbs 3:5–6 • Galatians 5:22–23 • Philippians 4:7

> "The LORD is my light and my
> salvation—whom shall I fear?
> The LORD is the stronghold of my
> life—of whom shall I be afraid?"
>
> PSALM 27:1

CONTEXT

The book of Psalms includes many types of poetry: praise psalms, royal psalms, psalms of lament, and psalms of thanksgiving. Psalm 27 is a psalm of both lament and praise.

MEANING

David starts Psalm 27 by declaring God's power over his enemies. He calls the Lord his light, his salvation, and his refuge against the adversaries who rise against him. In the midst of the ever-present danger of his season in the wilderness, David clings to God as his safe place. The imagery of God as a safe place continues throughout the psalm, as David trades his fear for the intimacy of God's holy presence, saying:

> "One thing I ask from the Lord, this only do I seek:
>   that I may dwell in the house of the Lord all the days of
> my life....
>   For in the day of trouble he will keep me safe in his
> dwelling;
>   he will hide me in the shelter of his sacred tent and set me
> high upon a rock" (vv. 4-5).

The intensity continues as David calls upon God to hear him and not reject him. He passionately asks the Lord to protect him from his enemies and lead him on the right path. But David's pleas are not made out of distrust; they are the cries of his heart, which beckon him to seek God's face, knowing that "Though my father and mother forsake me, the LORD will receive me" (v. 10).

APPLICATION

Because of the brokenness of the world, we all face personal "enemies" and "adversaries"—whether they be physical, spiritual, or emotional. This psalm reminds us of God's power and sovereignty over the hazards in our path. We can be confident in him no matter what life throws our way. The Lord is here for us. He is looking after us, and because of that, there is nothing we should fear. The final verses of Psalm 27 summarize the confidence we can have when we trust God with our lives: "I remain confident of this: I will see the goodness of the LORD in the land of the living. Wait for the LORD; be strong and take heart and wait for the LORD" (vv. 13-14).

ADDITIONAL READING

Psalm 62 • Romans 8:31

> "And God is able to bless you abundantly, so that in all things at all times, having all that you need, you will abound in every good work."
>
> 2 CORINTHIANS 9:8

CONTEXT

This letter to the church at Corinth from the apostle Paul is his most autobiographical and personal epistle. In it he rejoices over the improved situation at the church, which had struggled with division and false teaching, and defends his apostleship and message. Other themes include Christian giving and God's strength manifest in human weakness.

MEANING

Found in the passage in which Paul urges generous giving to the Macedonian church, verse 8 is a powerful, blanket assurance that believers need not worry they will be impoverished in any manner by liberal giving. It concisely conveys God's ability and will to keep blessings flowing to us so they can also flow through us—the will articulated in surrounding verses 6 and 10: "Whoever sows generously will also reap generously," and "Now he who supplies seed to the sower and bread for food will also supply and increase your store of seed and will enlarge the harvest of your righteousness."

The absoluteness of the verse marked by *alls* and *every*— "all things at all times," "all that you need," "every good work"—also should allay any fears about suffering a loss in giving.

APPLICATION

It is hard to give generously or cheerfully when you are worried about depleting your resources in doing so. Such worry, however, reveals a faulty view of yourself as a reservoir for God's blessing with a finite reserve, rather than as the infinitely supplied conduit depicted in 2 Corinthians 9:8. What remains, then, is to align your view with God's promise of provision and to "give what you have decided in your heart to give, not reluctantly or under compulsion, for God loves a cheerful giver" (v. 7). God has ordained and supplied us for good works (Ephesians 2:10); he will not let us run dry in the doing.

ADDITIONAL READING

Proverbs 11:24 • Proverbs 19:17 • 1 Corinthians 16:2

Luke 6:38 • Philippians 4:19

> "But the steadfast love of the Lord
> is from everlasting to everlasting
> on those who fear him, and his
> righteousness to children's children."
>
> PSALM 103:17 ESV

CONTEXT

Due to references to family and children, it is widely believed that David wrote Psalm 103 in his later years. He had the benefit of the perspective that age brings as he recorded these musings. What musings they would have been! Adventure! Victory! Fame! Power! Camaraderie! Great love! Many children! Wealth! And privilege! After all, he was a man after God's own heart.

It might be tempting for us to think that David, with all his brave and amazing accomplishments, did not ever feel afraid, become worried, or suffer from debilitating anxiety—that he wasn't like us. But you and I have the advantage of the perspective of David's journals, the psalms. That's the whole story, and countless times in them we watch as he cries out to our very same God in fear, frustration, discouragement, pain, anger, guilt, shame, doubt, worry, and anxiety.

MEANING

Verse 17 is nested in a stanza that describes the temporary nature of the length of a person's life and the fleeting influence we have when compared with the vast expanse of time.

We believers are familiar with the comparison of our lives to withering grass. Indeed, between our modern victories, we ourselves have daily struggles just like David did. How did the Lord answer David's pleas for help?

APPLICATION

When we are heavy with the load of cares that comes with a conscientious lifestyle; when we feel small and ineffective and beaten down; when we wonder if we will make it through or whether it's worth it, God offers hope in Psalm 103:17. He contrasts our temporary lives and current difficulties against his steadfast (resolutely or dutifully firm and unwavering) and everlasting (incessant; constantly recurring) love for us. Not only that, he promises to love our descendants too! What perspective! What comfort! What a loving Father!

ADDITIONAL READING

Deuteronomy 6:1–15 • Psalm 105 • Psalm 106

"Can all your worries add a single moment to your life? And why worry about your clothing? Look at the lilies of the field and how they grow. They don't work or make their clothing, yet Solomon in all his glory was not dressed as beautifully as they are."

MATTHEW 6:27–29 NLT

CONTEXT

Matthew 5–7 contains Jesus' Sermon on the Mount. This is one of Jesus' most well-known sermons. He was traveling through Galilee and, as crowds gathered around him, he went up on a mountainside to deliver his message, thus the name of this passage. Notable from these chapters are the Beatitudes, the Lord's Prayer, the Golden Rule, and many teachings on how to live a Christlike life. Relinquishing anxiety and worry is part of living like Christ. In the second half of Matthew 6, Jesus addresses this topic. Let's see what he says about it.

MEANING

Jesus poses a rational question in Matthew 6: Can anyone actually add even a single moment to their lives by worrying? No. Then why do we continue to worry about life's

circumstances and events? Somehow, we think worrying
will reveal an angle we haven't thought of, or that we can
gain some control over our situation. The truth is that only
Jesus is in control of and knows the outcome of what we walk
through.

Next, Jesus asks why we worry about our clothing. Jesus
adorns the wildflowers in beautiful bright colors and helps
them grow with sunshine and rainfall. King Solomon was a
wealthy and wise king, but even he wasn't dressed as mag-
nificently as the wildflowers. If Jesus cares enough to cover
the earth in gorgeous flowers and help them prosper, how
much more must he care about his children? He provides for
our every need, and he also loves to bless us with the desires
of our hearts. Jesus created us so that he could love us and
provide for us, which eliminates our need to worry. We are
more precious to him than anything else.

APPLICATION

Jesus meets you right where you're at no matter the circumstances. Surrender your worries to Jesus, then ask him for
peace that transcends understanding. He can provide that
kind of extraordinary peace. The Bible says so. Commit to
memorizing the below verses about the peace of Jesus and
recite them aloud when worries come knocking. Remember
that Jesus satisfies your every need, and he also loves to be-
stow you with amazing blessings. He's not going to let you
fall. You are safe and secure in his love.

ADDITIONAL READING

Isaiah 54:10 • Isaiah 58:11 • Philippians 4:6–7

> "The LORD is close to the
> brokenhearted and saves those
> who are crushed in spirit."
>
> PSALM 34:18

CONTEXT

Psalm 34 was written by David, who was the king of the nation of Israel. It's categorized as a psalm of thanksgiving, offering gratitude to God for something he's done. David wrote this passage after avoiding being captured by Abimelech, the leader of an opposing empire. David had been avoiding Abimelech and had spent much time alone, on the run, hiding in desolate caves and forests.

MEANING

In Psalm 34:17, David writes that "the righteous cry out, and the LORD hears them." In verse 18, the Lord saves those who are crushed in spirit. Both verses show that David wasn't afraid of surrender or humility, especially in times of danger or anguish. He cried out and trusted the Lord would save him and restore his spirit. For most of us, crying out goes against our natural desire to appear like we have control over a situation.

APPLICATION

The good news of Psalm 34 is that God desires to rescue us from whatever we're facing. When David declares that God

"saves those who are crushed in spirit," he dispels any no-
tions readers may have that David is talking only about physical danger. The psalm assures us that God promises to meet
us not just in the middle of danger but also in the middle of
pain. If you've given up hope and can't do much else, God
has not forgotten you. Call on the Lord, who knows what it
means to suffer deeply and who longs to lift your spirit with
his presence and nearness.

ADDITIONAL READING

Psalm 147:3 • Lamentations 3:25 • Isaiah 61:1

> "Come, everyone who is thirsty,
> come to the water; and you
> without silver, come, buy, and
> eat! Come, buy wine and milk
> without silver and without cost!"
>
> ISAIAH 55:1 CSB

CONTEXT

As a prophet of God, Isaiah urged people to decide: Will you believe God or not? Will you accept his invitation and trust him? Isaiah lived during the eighth century before Christ was born. He is the only author mentioned in the book that carries his name, but scholars generally believe that two of his disciples, perhaps more, helped to write the sixty-six chapters. The Old Testament book provides several prophecies of the coming Christ and, overall, points to our need for salvation.

MEANING

It is fitting that so much of Isaiah is focused on the Lord's saving power, for Isaiah's name means "the salvation of Yahweh." In chapter 12, he offers a song of praise with this especially reassuring verse: "Indeed, God is my salvation; I will trust him and not be afraid" (12:2 CSB).

Each of us has received the greatest invitation ever: to come to God with our sins and with our cares. Isaiah 55:1

makes it clear: "Come, everyone who is thirsty, come to the water; and you without silver, come, buy, and eat! Come, buy wine and milk without silver and without cost!"

So much of today's world is transactional. We pay money for goods and services. We do a favor for someone, and expect—or at least hope—they'll return the favor. That's not how it is with God though. If we thirst for his living water, if we need rescuing, he provides freely. All are welcome to his blessings.

APPLICATION

If stress or anxious feelings have left you empty or like you're not in good enough shape for God, fight back those thoughts. Resist the urge to withdraw from him. Remember that while Christ was on earth, he ministered to those in need—people who were in no position to "repay" him. Think of the blind man he healed, the wedding hosts at Cana, the paralyzed man whose sins he forgave.

Accept God's invitation as expressed in Isaiah 55:1. Pray and ask him for what you need. Enjoy the blessings of salvation—the water, the wine, and the milk that represent far more than physical sustenance. Our Savior already paid the cost when he died on the cross for us. Receive his grace freely.

ADDITIONAL READING

Matthew 5:6 • John 7:37 • Isaiah 44:3

> "But even if you should suffer
> for what is right, you are blessed.
> 'Do not fear their threats;
> do not be frightened.'"
>
> 1 PETER 3:14

CONTEXT

First Peter is a letter written by the apostle Peter to the Christians in several cities of modern-day Turkey. Peter was one of Jesus' closest friends during his earthly ministry, and after Jesus' resurrection, he became one of the most prominent leaders of the early church. The focal point of the letter is Jesus Christ himself.

MEANING

We've all suffered for wrong things we've done. When you're a kid, you might get punished for lying or talking back or fighting with your brother or sister. But have you ever suffered for doing what is right? That happens too, but it's so much harder to take. It's unjust, and injustice has a special sting to it.

In this chapter, Peter talks about many practical things. He begins by discussing husband and wife relationships and how men and women should conduct themselves. But then he makes a shift to talking about suffering. Namely, how to suffer well. We are told to be humble and rather than repay evil with evil, we are to repay evil with blessing.

How is such a thing possible? It goes against our very nature. Indeed, it does, which is why we must take on the nature of Christ.

But we also must keep in mind—if the world loves us and everyone is on our side, we're likely doing something wrong. The world hated Christ, and it will hate his followers as well. The verse for the day tells us that you are blessed when you suffer for good. Why? Because you are within the will of God.

All of this might mean very little if we didn't have this promise just a couple of verses earlier: "For the eyes of the Lord are on the righteous and his ears are attentive to their prayer, but the face of the Lord is against those who do evil" (v. 12). God is watching and is on your side.

APPLICATION

Is there anyone in your life who means you harm? Or perhaps a cultural system or belief that is working against you despite the fact that you're trying to fight for what is right? Take courage. God is watching and you are blessed. Pray for strength, peace, and humility.

ADDITIONAL READING

2 Corinthians 4:17 • 2 Timothy 3:12 • Isaiah 43:2

> "Delight yourself in the LORD,
> and he will give you the
> desires of your heart."
>
> PSALM 37:4 ESV

CONTEXT

David wrote Psalm 37 as an acrostic poem; that is, each stanza of this song begins with a letter of the Hebrew alphabet. It's important to note that it is a teaching psalm, directed at man, not God. Perhaps this style was used as a memorization tool, something easy to recall in one's own heart when remembering the Lord's ways.

MEANING

In the first third of Psalm 37, David is offering counsel and encouragement for the afflicted people of God. He is answering the problem of evil in the world and specifically addressing the idea that evildoers seem to flourish. It is a common thing for the righteous to become anxious when we see evil prosper. Those who have followed the Lord are indeed familiar with the sting of watching unbelievers appear to be happy in their sin. "Why is that?" we ask ourselves. While we, who are committed to obedience, wait to feed on his faithfulness, the unrighteous seem to succeed.

APPLICATION

The verses just before this one tell us that the wrongdoers will fade and wither like grass. Their satisfaction is temporary just as man's life is temporary. It is God who is eternal and who offers eternal life. This long-term view is an important concept to keep in mind. We don't live to satisfy our earthly desires; we live to follow our Father, who provides for our needs and wants as he sees fit.

This verse is redirecting our attention from those around us who don't know or follow God's ways to remember to delight in the Lord instead. When we look to him, expecting what he offers us—truth, goodness, faithfulness, as seen in the verse just before this one—then he shall give us the desires of our heart. As followers of our loving God, by now we've realized that his ways are higher than the world's. When we look to him, desire him, he resets our priorities to align with his own. Peace comes to our hearts and minds when we refocus our gaze on our just Father, instead of the evil around us. He allows us the ability to delight, and he satisfies us there.

ADDITIONAL READING

Psalm 55:22 • Proverbs 16:3 • Luke 12:22

2 Corinthians 4:18 • 1 Peter 5:7

> "There is no fear in love. But perfect love drives out fear, because fear has to do with punishment. The one who fears is not made perfect in love."
>
> 1 JOHN 4:18

CONTEXT

The book of 1 John was written to encourage and assure the local church after some in the church began to drift away from God's truth. These leaders became false teachers who tried to convert others to their way of thinking. John wrote these three letters to speak the truth about who Jesus is and why he came.

MEANING

In Dante's epic poem *The Divine Comedy*, he talks about love being the power that runs the universe. Good things are motivated and caused by love. Bad things are some type of perversion of love. Love is the center of all things, and nothing happens without it.

The focus of the passage that today's verse comes from is also love. We are told to love one another because love comes from God. Indeed, God is love. These three words— "God is love"—may be among the most powerful words ever uttered. If we truly understand what love is, understanding these words will change us. So how are we supposed to define love? The passage tells us that it's based on his sacrificing his

Son for us. Love is sacrifice. Love is willingness to suffer for another.

That sort of love—that sacrificial kind that is willing to suffer for the beloved—has no room for fear. If God loved us enough to send his Son, what is there to be afraid of? Surely not God! He suffered for us. God is above all, and nothing is more powerful than he. So that leaves us with no options left. Fear and love just don't mix.

But the passage doesn't leave us there—it calls us to higher things. If this is how God loves us, we must love others similarly. That is a high calling indeed.

APPLICATION

When you think of love, do you think of sacrifice? Thank God for his sacrifice on your behalf. Then meditate on how the most powerful being in the universe was willing to suffer for you. Pray that God helps you catch a glimpse of this love and that it would wipe away your fear.

ADDITIONAL READING

Romans 8:32 • Romans 8:37–39 • Isaiah 54:10

> "It is useless for you to work
> so hard from early morning
> until late at night, anxiously
> working for food to eat; for God
> gives rest to his loved ones."
>
> PSALM 127:2 NLT

CONTEXT

Psalm 127 is often recognized by the first verse, "Unless the LORD builds a house . . . " which refers to Jesus being the foundation of all of our pursuits. Unless we place Jesus at the center of our activities, our "house-building" won't be successful and we work in vain. Verse 2 takes this wisdom further by advising us to rest and allow Jesus to provide.

MEANING

Although in this context the word *house* is synonymous with *family,* the principles apply to other areas of life. We know that we need a strong foundation in Jesus. This is the best way for us to build anything that we seek in life. But what about how hard we work toward our own goals—our own labor? Verse 2 says that it is useless for us to anxiously work hard for long hours. *Anxiously* implies that we rely on ourselves rather than on Jesus to provide. Difficult and lengthy work doesn't ensure our prosperity or security, especially if we haven't centered our work in the Lord.

The last part of verse 2 promises rest from the Lord. Rest from your labor also means rest in the knowledge that Jesus freely gives provision. Jesus will provide for your needs, and he'll bless you with rest. Our culture thrives on the busyness of life with people wearing their activities like a badge of honor. Rest has become an elusive thing of the past. However, rest is a gift, "for God gives rest to his loved ones." Jesus doesn't want us anxiously overworking. He longs to give us stillness, calm, and sleep, which are necessary for our health and for our souls.

APPLICATION

The next time you're tempted to push yourself beyond capacity, examine your motives. Do you have a deadline that you're working to meet, or are you fearful that you won't have enough or be enough unless you trudge forward? If it's the latter, confess your doubts to the Lord and commit to sign off as often as possible. Stick to a daily quiet time with Jesus and see how the consistency shifts your mindset. Lastly, find pockets of peace in your weeks and let the tranquility seep in and restore your soul.

ADDITIONAL READING

Genesis 2:2–3 • Psalm 46:10

Matthew 11:28–30 • Colossians 3:23

> "For we know that if the tent that is our earthly home is destroyed, we have a building from God, a house not made with hands, eternal in the heavens."
>
> 2 CORINTHIANS 5:1 ESV

CONTEXT

The apostle Paul reveals much about himself in his letters to the Corinthians—personal experiences of suffering for Christ and a mysterious thorn in his flesh. His second letter admonishes the church at Corinth to lay aside offense, practice forgiveness, mend division, and be about the work of spreading the gospel. Paul is setting up a perspective adjustment: We will all one day perish. Our difficulties are temporary, and we are promised an eternal home. What a way to get the reader's attention and drive home the facts. We have all sinned and fallen short. We are all saved by his grace. We have a great promise to live toward. And we are mandated to share about it with others.

MEANING

But we get distracted. We become heavy-laden with the way of this world. Many people—believers and nonbelievers—are worried about the temporariness of our earthly bodies. Death bothers us—who wants to talk about their body being destroyed?! Some of us fear death itself, while others are anxious about the unknown existence beyond it. Some are troubled by the idea that death might be painful. Still others of us might be reticent to admit that we secretly welcome death since we unfortunately suffer from ailments and difficulties in this tent of our earthly home. Our circumstances span a range of temporary discomfort to excruciating pain to chronic, lifelong conditions. Lord, have mercy on us.

APPLICATION

But we, Christ followers, have the tremendous opportunity to trust Jesus' own promises about how we will one day live together with him in heaven. This is the blessed assurance! Paul reminds us of it here in these verses.

He is Lord of it all. Lord of our bodies though they be temporary as tents in the desert. Lord of our hearts as we combat fear, worry, and anxiety over the issues of this life. Lord of our experiences as we navigate pitfalls, injustices, and frustrations.

Our Father asks us to take the long view. He reminds us it's all temporary, and promises he is building a house for us with him in paradise—heaven, our eternal home. Something inside us resonates with this certainty, for we are, after all, created for union with God. May his peace fill us up today as we look on his beautiful provision for us, remembering Christ's sacrifice that made it just so. May the promise of an eternal existence with God in heaven replace the discomfort of today's afflictions.

ADDITIONAL READING

John 14:2–3   •   1 Corinthians 2:9   •   Philippians 3:13

2 Timothy 1:10   •   Revelation 21:4

"At this, Job got up and tore his robe
    and shaved his head. Then he fell
    to the ground in worship and said:
'Naked I came from my mother's
    womb,
    and naked I will depart.
The Lord gave and the Lord has taken
    away;
    may the name of the Lord be
    praised.'"

JOB 1:20–21

CONTEXT

The book of Job presents the story of a righteous man whom
God allows to be tested by Satan. His property is destroyed,
children are killed, and health fails. While friends gather to
comfort him—with mixed results—Job maintains his faith
(despite struggles), and in the end, God blesses him once
again.

MEANING

According to many pastors and scholars, the main theme of
Job is "theodicy," which is the question of why there is evil
if God is good. Job suffered greatly, but why? According to

chapter 1, it was because he was righteous. He was "blameless" and "upright" and honored God with sacrifices.

Job mourned his losses, as well he should. But he also
blessed God's name. He realized that if we're going to accept
good things from God, we also need to accept the bad.

So why did God let him be attacked by Satan? The answer, it turns out, never comes. What we discover by the end
of the book is that God doesn't owe us an answer. We are
only assured that he is watching, and nothing happens that
he doesn't allow. But the formula of why bad things happen
to good people is never shown.

Thankfully, even though we never get a complete answer
to why God does the things he does, we do get a satisfactory
conclusion. God blesses Job. By the end of the book, he has
more than he'd ever had before. Is that guaranteed in this
life? No. But our lives don't end here on earth. We can rest in
the fact that God is just, he loves us, and in the end, he will
bless his people.

APPLICATION

Have things happened to you that you just don't understand?
Have you been punished for doing the right thing and obeying God? This is unjust, and it's all right to mourn. But it is
also good to praise him in the suffering. God deserves your
praise, through the good times and the bad. But it is also for
your own good. It reminds you that God is in charge and is
bigger than your circumstances, and that in the end, he will
bless his children.

ADDITIONAL READING

2 Corinthians 4:17 • 2 Corinthians 1:3–4

Deuteronomy 8:3

> "If I go and prepare a place
> for you, I will come back and
> take you to be with me that you
> also may be where I am."
>
> JOHN 14:3

CONTEXT

The Gospel of John was written by the apostle John, one of the first followers of Jesus. He was with Jesus from the early days of Jesus' ministry through the time of his ascension into heaven. John tells us that Jesus comforted the disciples with the words of John 14:3 just after the Last Supper on the night before he was crucified.

MEANING

In John 14:2, Jesus says, "My Father's house has many rooms; if that were not so, would I have told you that I am going there to prepare a place for you?" This would have reminded the disciples of Jewish wedding customs. After a man and woman became betrothed, the man went to his father's house to add a room for him and his future bride to live in. He was gone for several months, or even years, in order to "prepare a place" for her. When the room was ready, he returned, they were married, and he took her to his father's house.

In several places, the Bible compares Christ and the church to a bride and bridegroom. Just like a Jewish bridegroom, Jesus has gone to prepare a place for us, and when he returns, he will take us to be with him. We don't know how long it will be until he returns, but we can trust that he will. And when he does, we will go with him to heaven, which is an actual physical place where all the pain and difficulties of this world will be behind us.

Jesus tells us not to let our hearts be troubled, but to trust him (John 14:1). He will do what he has promised to do.

APPLICATION

Brides in Jesus' day didn't know when their bridegrooms would return for them, and we don't know when Jesus will return for us. But we can trust that he will return, and we must be ready when he does.

When we experience difficulties here on earth, we can take comfort in knowing that no matter what happens, our struggles here won't last. One day Jesus will return to take us with him, and we'll leave all our earthly troubles behind. If we choose to remember that the Lord is preparing a place for us where we can be with him for eternity, we can focus on our future rather than our problems.

ADDITIONAL READING

Matthew 25:1–13 • John 3:29 • Acts 1:11

Revelation 19:7

"God will wipe away every tear from their eyes; there shall be no more death, nor sorrow, nor crying. There shall be no more pain, for the former things have passed away."

REVELATION 21:4 NKJV

CONTEXT

The apostle John wrote the book of Revelation after having a vision on the island of Patmos, where he had been exiled due to his Christian beliefs and ministry. In his vision, he hears declarations from the throne of God. One of the declarations is this verse, which may be the most encouraging in all of Scripture.

MEANING

There's so much pain in this world. People suffer from diseases, hunger, physical and emotional abuse, accidents, injustice, persecution, war, and all kinds of natural disasters. It's easy to wonder how God could let it all happen.

But God is not the creator of any of it. It all entered the world when Satan tempted mankind to sin in Genesis chapter 3. The rest of the Bible is the story of God's work to redeem us from our sin and put an end to all pain and suffering.

He reached out to Abraham to create a nation that would follow him and bless all the other nations. He brought them out of slavery in Egypt. He blessed them when they followed him, and he corrected them when they strayed from him again and again. Finally, he sent his Son to die for our sins and give us eternal life.

Sin is the source of all our pain, and Jesus died to forgive our sin. In heaven, sin will be no more, so pain will be no more. Suffering will be no more. Death will be no more.

APPLICATION

In difficult times, there are many things we can turn to for help: Counseling, medication, exercise, eating healthier, physical therapy, and support groups can all improve our well-being. But none of these solutions lasts forever. Our God is the only one who declares the end of crying, sorrow, and death.

Imagine, one day all your tears will be gone. There will be no more suffering of any kind—no more death, no more disease, no more pain. May it encourage you today to know that no matter what difficulty you're struggling with, it will end. God will be victorious. He will wipe every tear from your eyes.

ADDITIONAL READING

Isaiah 25:8 • Psalm 56:8 • Revelation 20:14

> "[F]rom the end of the earth I call to you when my heart is faint. Lead me to the rock that is higher than I...."
>
> PSALM 61:2 ESV

CONTEXT

The 150 chapters of the Psalms are attributed to seven different writers, with close to half of them (including chapter 61) attributed to David. Psalm 61 includes both pleas for help and declarations of worship, and starts with a note that it was meant to be sung with stringed instruments.

MEANING

David begins chapter 61 with a plea of desperation, asking God to hear his cries. In verse 2 he says he is calling out "from the end of the earth," indicating he feels alone and isolated from God. He asks God to bring him "to the rock that is higher than I." A rock is both a symbol of strength and immovability—something that easily contradicts how David is feeling—as well as a symbol of safety. In a flood, higher ground is of course preferable, as is higher ground when under attack from an enemy army, since higher ground allows for more visibility of the enemy and less accessibility for capture. Simply put, a higher rock is strong and safe. In saying that God is "the rock that is higher," David is admitting the inherent gospel truth that God is strong and he, David, is not. He needs the Lord to help him, for he cannot succeed on his own. This theme continues into verse 3, where David speaks of the Lord as his "refuge" and "strong tower against the enemy." David ends the chapter by saying that the Lord "heard my vows" (61:5) and sings praises to the Lord. David gives us a glimpse of a God who gives us safety and rest in our weakness.

APPLICATION

Hope can be gleaned from coming to the same realization that David came to—that he, as a human, is weak, but that the Lord is powerful and able to give us the safety and rest he couldn't achieve on his own. While it may initially feel discouraging to realize that we can't do it (after all, that is not a sentiment often used in encouraging greeting cards), the truth is that God can, and that instills hope. God is not human. God is not weak. He hears and answers our cries. We don't need to strive so hard to be self-sufficient when the chaos threatens to overwhelm us, but we can rest in the truth that God is infinitely more capable than we are.

ADDITIONAL READING

Proverbs 3:5–6 • Isaiah 40:31 • Isaiah 41:10

Psalm 34:18 • Psalm 27:5

> "What, then, shall we say in response to these things? If God is for us, who can be against us?"
>
> ROMANS 8:31

CONTEXT

Paul wrote this letter to the churches of Rome, explaining the revelation of God's judgment through the law and saving grace through Christ's redemptive work on the cross, while addressing theological questions and concerns of the early church. Paul discusses that we are dead to sin, alive to Christ, living by the Spirit, and a part of future glory to be revealed.

MEANING

Our suffering is "not worth comparing with the glory that will be revealed in us" (v. 18). God predestined us and called us. Therefore, no snare of the enemy will ever succeed because he works it for his glory. The chapter continues to declare we are more than conquerors, and nothing is able to separate us from the love of God. So who can be against us if the all-knowing God of the universe is for us? The chapter goes on to ask, "Who will bring any charge against those whom God has chosen?" The everlasting love of the Creator God is on our side and working all things for the good; therefore, the enemy will not prevail. We know the end of the story and the victory Jesus has already won.

APPLICATION

God is greater than our daily temptation and larger than the opposition we face; we have ultimate victory in Christ.

It can be easy to want approval of humanity or believe that everything should go our way. But that is not what the Bible says. Trials and tribulation will come, but we have the promises of God to stand on. This verse is one of those promises.

Death, betrayal, job loss, fear, sickness, a mistake—all of these things God can work for good. It can produce good fruit, it can open new doors, and it can bring glory to the Father. Isn't that good news?

Our God is for us. He is the conductor of the orchestra, the painter of the masterpiece. The God of the universe is for us. He is not trying to trick you; he is for you. He is not condemning you; he is for you. He has not forgotten you; he is for you. No matter what tomorrow brings, you can rejoice, because he is for you.

ADDITIONAL READING

Isaiah 54:17 • John 1:5 • 1 Corinthians 15:57

> "Even though I walk through the darkest valley, I will fear no evil, for you are with me; your rod and your staff, they comfort me."
>
> PSALM 23:4

CONTEXT

"The Lord is my shepherd!" How many times in your life have you heard those words? Psalm 23 offers a unique perspective because David, the author, served as a shepherd in his youth before becoming king. He knew firsthand what it meant to be the shepherd of sheep, and then later in life a shepherd of people. Shepherds live with their flock and are intimately involved in daily life. Like David to his sheep and his people, Jesus is our shepherd and walks through each moment alongside us.

MEANING

This psalm is peaceful, but it covers the spectrum: green meadows, peaceful streams, right paths, and darkest valleys. We have all heard this psalm used as a comfort for those facing trials. It addresses the calm and turbulent moments in life as well as God's provision. All of us will likely encounter "dark valleys" in our lives. These dark valleys can appear as death, illness, anxiety, depression, fear, or worry. Our promise is this: We will not be afraid. Our shepherd's rod and staff will comfort us.

Dark valleys don't stay dark. The beauty of a valley is that it dips down but then rises back up. Valleys aren't endless stretches of defeat, but stretches that we walk through and rise from. What a beautiful promise. We are not alone in our valleys. Even as we "walk through," we don't need to sprint through in a panic; we will walk through our valleys with Jesus by our side and emerge safely, made stronger by the experience.

APPLICATION

Trials or dark valleys are intimidating. However, we can move through them without fear because Jesus will shepherd us along and protect us from harm. Memorize Psalm 23 and recite it the next time you face something unsettling. Life isn't only full of valleys. Hills and mountains wait on the other side. Not only will Jesus walk with you, but he will also provide you rest in green meadows, lead you beside peaceful streams, and guide you along right paths.

ADDITIONAL READING

Psalm 27:5 • Isaiah 41:10 • Isaiah 43:2

> ## "Then you will know the truth, and the truth will set you free."
>
> JOHN 8:32

CONTEXT

As mentioned in previous chapters, the book of John was written by the apostle John, one of Jesus' closest friends while on his earthly ministry. It is believed that this was the last of the Gospels to be written. In chapter 20, John states that the book was written "that you may believe that Jesus is the Messiah, the Son of God, and that by believing you may have life in his name" (v. 31).

MEANING

Do you ever feel trapped by your fears? As if you can't get away from them regardless of what you do? They just keep coming back, tormenting you with thoughts of calamity or worries about what the future holds?

Jesus wants to set you free!

In this section of John chapter 8, Jesus is speaking to the Pharisees and other Jews. After telling them that he is God's very Son, some of them believed. To these believing Jews, Jesus said, "If you hold to my teaching, you will know the truth, and the truth will set you free."

But free from what? Jesus answers that question two verses later: "Everyone who sins is a slave to sin." Jesus says that knowing the truth and holding to his teaching will set us free from sin. But what does that have to do with anxiety and worry, the themes of this book? Right after Jesus talks about being a slave to sin, he says that a slave is not part of the family. In other words, when the truth sets us free from sin, it also sets us in the Father's family forever. And being in that family is the source of peace and the only way we can be free of fear. A slave is treated as property, whereas a family member is loved. Which one do you think has a reason to be fearful?

APPLICATION

Sometimes we forget that sin is the opposite of freedom. We think sin is freedom to do as we want, but it's really a prison that keeps us from God. Focus on God's truth today and holding on to Jesus' teaching. Are there any areas of your life where you've been ignoring him? Confess those and remind yourself that he forgives and that you're a member of his family forever.

ADDITIONAL READING

Romans 8:1–4 • Galatians 4:3–7

> "Say to those who have an anxious heart, 'Be strong; fear not! Behold, your God will come with vengeance, with the recompense of God. He will come and save you.'"
>
> ISAIAH 35:4 ESV

CONTEXT

Isaiah was a prophet who provided wisdom and vision to the people of Judah and Israel. At this point in time, Israel had been out of the promised land for nearly seven hundred years. The people of Israel had developed a civil war between themselves and became divided into two nations—Israel (to the north) and Judah (to the south). Prior to the beginning of Isaiah's ministry as a prophet, the Northern nation had gone through eighteen different kings, all of whom had rebelled against the Lord. The Southern nation wasn't much better, having eleven kings who were almost as rebellious as the others. When Isaiah enters the story, Israel was about to be overrun by Assyria, and Judah was facing threat from the surrounding nations.

MEANING

In Isaiah 34 he announces a terrible judgment that is coming to the nations of Israel and Judah. The people of Judah had lost their temple, their land, and their sovereignty.

Everything that gave them a sense of direction and purpose is completely lost. They are feeling distant from God. And right in the middle of that despair, there is a message of hope—Isaiah 35. In verse 2, Isaiah states that the dry desert will soon blossom, and it will blossom with abundance, joy, and singing. Creation will rejoice as it's restored! God has the power to transform creation, and he has the power to transform us too. We can never be too far gone that God won't invite us back to him. We can never be too broken that he can't restore us.

APPLICATION

For those feeling lost and far from home, for those facing a hard situation or circumstance, it's easy to forget who God is and the power he has in our lives. We see in Isaiah 35 that God cares deeply about an entire nation and for the trembling hearts of his people. As you read through Isaiah and the rest of Scripture, you will come to understand that God DOES invite us back to him and DOES offer restoration to our lives. Just like the people of Israel and Judah, we do not need to fear, because we have God on our side. Be strong, fear not! Salvation comes from the Lord, and he has come to save us!

ADDITIONAL READING

Hebrews 12:12 • Matthew 11:4–6 • Revelation 21:4

> "So we say with confidence,
> 'The Lord is my helper; I will not be
>   afraid.
> What can mere mortals do to
>   me?'"
>
> HEBREWS 13:6

CONTEXT

The book of Hebrews was written to Jewish believers in Christ, encouraging them to remain faithful to Jesus rather than return to Judaism. The book shows that Jesus is greater than Moses, Aaron, angels, prophets, and priests. Chapter 13 is filled with practical advice on hospitality, marriage, and submission to authority.

MEANING

This verse begins with the word *so*, which means to understand it, you need to read the previous verse. The previous verse ends with the promise from God: "Never will I leave you; never will I forsake you," which is a quote from Deuteronomy. It's easy to see why this would lead naturally to the confident statement, "The Lord is my helper; I will not be afraid." That is also a quote from the Old Testament, but this time from Psalm 118. These promises were so important, God decided to put them in Scripture twice!

God is your helper. Let that sink in for a moment. We all need help at times—whether from our parents, our friends, our colleagues, or even from the government. But all these other helpers will at times let us down. They're just not big enough, powerful enough, or loving enough to always help us in the ways we need. But the infinite, omnipotent God will never let you down. Another passage in Scripture says, "The arm of the LORD is not too short," meaning he's powerful enough for any task.

Interestingly, if we go back just a little further in Hebrews 13:5, we discover that the context to God's promise to never leave us is about money and contentment: Don't love money, and be content with what you have. Why? Because God promises to never leave you or forsake you. And that leads to fearlessness. How often money, or the lack thereof, keeps us up at night. Will we have enough to provide for ourselves and our families? What happens if we get another unexpected bill?

But God's arm is not short. He can always reach into his pockets to provide.

APPLICATION

Is the lack of money a source of fear for you? Pray for contentment, holding on to the promise that God will never leave you or forsake you. Then trust in God as your helper and let your fear pass away. Pray this Scripture to yourself, claiming these promises from God.

ADDITIONAL READING

Psalm 118   •   Deuteronomy 31   •   Isaiah 59:1

> "But whoever listens to me
> will live in safety and be at
> ease, without fear of harm."
>
> PROVERBS 1:33

CONTEXT

Much of the book of Proverbs was written by King Solomon, the son of David. It is a collection of practical wisdom that is organized into pithy, memorable statements. The key word is *practical*, in that most of the verses focus on how to wisely live one's everyday life rather than wrestling with the big questions about the relationship between God and man.

MEANING

The first chapter of Proverbs gives general advice on living wisely, and the emphasis is on humbly listening to the right voices. We all fail to listen sometimes, and quite often it's because of pride. We think we know best. This chapter, on the other hand, emphasizes the humility of listening to God and fearing him rather than assuming we have it figured out on our own.

The highlighted verse for today is within a passage spoken by a female personification of wisdom. In other words, the idea of "wisdom" is given a personality here, and she's calling out to us to listen to her voice.

Verse 33 makes a bold claim: If you listen to her (wisdom), you will live in safety, live an easy life, and have no reason to fear. Is this true? Yes, it's true because it's in the Bible. On the other hand, other places in the Bible say that trouble comes to everyone. How can both things be true? To answer that, we have to consider the point of Proverbs: to give people practical instruction. For instance, if you tell your child to study hard so they can get a good job, are you promising that they'll never be out of work or won't struggle with their career? Of course not. But is it true that studying hard is a path to better employment? Absolutely! In other words, pointing out cause and effect relationships (being wise leads to less fear) is not the same as a biblical promise. But it's still sound and true!

APPLICATION

Most of the other verses in this book contain promises from God. This one, on the other hand, gives sound advice— which isn't quite the same thing.

Take a moment to think about your own life. Are there things you're doing that are unwise? Maybe there is sin that you haven't dealt with, bad spending habits, an unhealthy lifestyle, etc. Working on these things can help you live a less anxious or worried life. Pray that God helps you see any actions you could take to clear a path for more peace and less anxiety.

ADDITIONAL READING

James 3:17   •   Matthew 7:24–27

> "And let the peace of Christ
> rule in your hearts, to which
> indeed you were called in one
> body. And be thankful."
>
> COLOSSIANS 3:15 ESV

CONTEXT

In Colossians 1:1–2 we learn that the book is a letter to the Christians at Colossae written by Paul and Timothy. The church at Colossae started while Paul was in Ephesus, so while he may have never visited Colossae, Paul feels a sense of pastorship toward the people there. He writes a letter with Timothy (some scholars believe Timothy was transcribing for Paul) to encourage the Colossians in their newfound faith and to provide instructions on living a Christlike life. Chapter 3 focuses on specific ways to "put on the new self" and change their behavior from "the old self" (3:9) now that they have Christ. Verses 8–16 focus on being Christlike in relationships with others—Paul and Timothy instruct the Colossians to be kind, humble, and to forgive one another.

MEANING

Because of the context of the previous few verses, verse 15 continues the theme of loving and getting along with others. If we allow "the peace of Christ" to rule our hearts, we will be able to achieve unity with other believers. In order for our relationships to be transformed by this peace, the peace needs to first rule in us and over our thought life. In the same way that having Christ's peace rule our hearts changes how we interact with others, having Christ's peace also changes how we interact with ourselves and respond to the world around us. If we are focused on the peace Christ has given us, everything else that flows out of us—our thoughts, words, and actions—will have an undertone of peace rather than an undertone of fear or worry. This is the image Paul instructs us to strive toward.

APPLICATION

Stress, worry, and anxiety (and the innumerable situations that cause those things) threaten to upend the peace in our hearts, but Paul encourages us to allow the peace of Christ to live in our hearts even still. If our thoughts are normally a chaotic collection of worries throughout the day, focusing on this peace and the hope of being Christlike can help us combat those thoughts. Achieving peace is not an easy goal, but it is possible with the new life that we have in Christ.

The verse ends with the simple yet powerful directive to "be thankful." Gratefulness is often a common tactic used to combat worry or negative thinking, and for good reason—it works! If we are focused on thanking God for the ways in which he has provided, our focus is not on our worries. This is not only a useful technique toward healthy thinking— being thankful is a biblical mandate. Creating a lifestyle of thankfulness can help us to obtain the peace of Christ that Paul speaks of.

ADDITIONAL READING

Proverbs 4:23 • Hebrews 6:19 • Philippians 4:6–7

John 14:27 • John 16:33 • Isaiah 26:3

James 1:17 • Psalm 100:4–5

> "I am the good shepherd.
> The good shepherd lays down
> his life for the sheep."
>
> JOHN 10:11

CONTEXT

The book of John was written by the apostle John, one of
Jesus' closest friends during his earthly ministry. It is believed that this was the last of the Gospels to be written. In
chapter 20, John states that the book was written "that you
may believe that Jesus is the Messiah, the Son of God, and
that by believing you may have life in his name."

MEANING

To understand the meaning of John chapter 10, we have to
back up to the previous chapter. In John 9, Jesus has just
healed a man who was blind from birth. This was quite the
scandal, supposedly because Jesus healed him on the Sab-
bath day, but more likely because the Pharisees were jealous
of Jesus' power and authority. Chapter 9 ends with Jesus in a
dispute with some Pharisees because Jesus accuses them of
being guilty of sin.

From there, chapter 10 focuses on Jesus as the Good
Shepherd. This is in contrast to the spiritual and political
leaders of his time, whom Jesus is equating to thieves and
robbers. Why? Because they don't really care for the sheep.
They just want to use them for their own ends.

Jesus, on the other hand, sacrifices all for his sheep. Verse 11 couldn't be more clear: Jesus, the Good Shepherd, is willing to give his life for his sheep. And this was no idle promise—he was predicting his own terrible death for our sakes.

As it says in Isaiah chapter 53, we are all like sheep who have strayed from the right path, and God laid on Jesus our sins. He, the Good Shepherd, fulfilled his own prophecy on the cross.

The passage goes on from there to distinguish between hired hands, who would just run away if a wolf comes to take a sheep, and the good shepherd, who would lay down his own life to save them. From there he talks about his sheep knowing his voice.

APPLICATION

We fret and worry because we believe it's our responsibility to look out for ourselves. If we don't, who will? Jesus, of course. Our Good Shepherd laid down his very life for his sheep, proving a love that is deeper than we can understand. He is calling you to lay down your burdens and trust in him.

Trust in Jesus as your Good Shepherd—not only for your salvation but for the daily struggles in your life. Even as a Christian, it is easy to start following robbers and hired hands. Listen carefully for the voice of your shepherd and go where he leads. There you will always be safe.

ADDITIONAL READING

Isaiah 53 • Psalm 23

> "But God shows his love
> for us in that while we were still
> sinners, Christ died for us."
>
> ROMANS 5:8 ESV

CONTEXT

In the apostle Paul's letter to the Romans, Paul firmly tells this congregation that everyone is in need of Jesus. This letter is a call for both Jews and Gentiles to be faithful to Jesus Christ just as Christ is faithful to God.

MEANING

Taking this in three parts, let's discuss "God shows his love for us" first. Love is not just an emotion you feel toward your family or your friends. In fact, it is so much more than just emotional. And the love God has for you and me is far greater than even that. God loves us emotionally, of course, but the showing of that love, the grace that he gives, is what ultimately drives us toward him.

"While we were still sinners" expresses the irrevocability of God's love for us. Every day when we choose to follow anything other than God, we are sinning against him. When our minds are filled with worries, doubts, and fears, we are forgetting that only the Lord is worthy of our fear. Because even in our darkest moments and even with our deepest sins, he is going to choose us and love us.

However, the only sacrifice big enough to cover our sins was Jesus' death on the cross. "Christ died for us" because he wanted to be in a relationship with us for eternity. Jesus did not want us to suffer, so he suffered for us. The depth of his love for you is impossible to understand. But know this: Jesus did not die on the cross so that you would be lonely or worried or anxious. Jesus died on the cross to be in relationship with you forever. And this is good news!

APPLICATION

When worry piles on top of worry and anxiety starts to spiral, it can be hard to praise God for his goodness. Today, give all your praise to the one who made you! Be reminded of the love God has for you—a love so great that he gave his only Son to die on the cross for you.

Once you begin to offer praise and worship, you will start to see the blessings he has given you in life. Seek out those blessings. Praise God for his grace when you see it. Find peace in knowing that you are greatly loved.

ADDITIONAL READING

Mark 10:27 • Luke 1:33 • John 8:12

> "Now may the Lord of peace
> Himself continually grant you
> peace in every circumstance.
> The Lord be with you all!"
>
> 2 THESSALONIANS 3:16 NASB

CONTEXT

This verse comes at the conclusion of Paul's second letter to the believers in Thessalonica, now known as Thessaloniki, Greece, which at the time of Paul's writing was the capital city in the Roman province of Macedonia. Paul addresses both exciting and difficult circumstances in his letters to these believers. In the context of this second one, Paul has just finished discussing church discipline and the rather delicate issue of how to treat rebellious believers within the church family. Yet here he turns to his hope for peace in every circumstance.

MEANING

There are some very encouraging points in this brief verse. First of all, Paul clearly defines the source of peace: our God and our Lord Jesus Christ. Then he adds the adverb *continually*. In the same way that he encouraged believers to "pray without ceasing" in 1 Thessalonians 5:17, here Paul prays that the Lord of peace will continually grant the believers peace.

This statement becomes even stronger with the phrase "in every circumstance." Paul's expression of this prayer and blessing is evidence of his confidence in Christ to bring it to fruition. As believers in Christ, we can rest in the hope that his peace and presence are with us in all circumstances.

Today, the word *peace* is so often used flippantly in a variety of contexts that it has been cheapened in our everyday vocabulary. The peace that Paul writes about here is a deep and transcendent peace. It is a lasting peace, a persistent peace, a peace flowing from the Lord of peace himself. What a blessing it is that we can live and walk within his presence and his peace.

APPLICATION

This identity in our Lord's peace parallels Jesus' Sermon on the Mount. In Matthew 5:9 (NASB), he states, "Blessed are the peacemakers, for they will be called sons of God." Not only is God the source and bringer of our peace, but we are also able to share in this blessing and have the privilege of seeing it become a part of our identity as sons and daughters of God. Because the Lord of peace is with us, we too are to be peacemakers.

ADDITIONAL READING

1 Thessalonians 5:16–18 • Matthew 5:1–11 • Psalm 34:14

> "The LORD will vindicate me;
> your love, Lord, endures forever
> —do not abandon the
> works of your hands."
>
> PSALM 138:8

CONTEXT

Psalm 138 is a thank-you letter to God for sending help and affirming his love in a time of need. When we thank God for what he has done, we may be comforted because he will never be finished doing the good works of his hands, presently or in the future.

MEANING

"Love": What a beautiful reminder of who God is and what he longs to do—love. Love is his way of cleansing hearts that ache with fear and worry. Pray: Pour your love on me, Lord. Wash me in torrents of love that refresh my soul.

"Endures": Do not fear that God's control over circumstances or his outpouring of love will ever stop. He will always and frequently be the portion we need. We are to rest when we are exhausted—he will carry us on. Pray: Lord, I surrender my life to you. You love to endure on my behalf.

"Forever": It is a good reminder to check our perspective. When our soul is fixed on Jesus, circumstances are seen for what they are: temporary. Fear and anxiety are real emotions, and there is a way through them. God's hands may

shield us like a strong tower. He may empower us to defeat
negative emotions with his own words (Scripture). He may
wash them away and fill the free space with more of himself.
He may change our perspective and the way we feel instantly
or walk beside us for each and every step. Our experience is
only temporary.

APPLICATION

Sometimes when circumstances and feelings are overwhelming, small bites packed with nutrition are all the body can
absorb. Here are healthy thoughts on just four words:

"Your love endures forever." Four bites; we can do that!

"Your": This is a possessive word; it means "belonging
to." As the Lord is sovereign, any circumstance is under his
authority. As a Christ follower, we have the Father who declares that fear and anxiety are not part of the family; they
are not related to us. Surrender these characters to the Lord,
who will take action against them with his capable hands.
Pray: Abba (Daddy), I put fear and anxiety in your hands.
You, Jesus, are the Lord of my heart. You will not leave me
unfinished, living with fear and worry. Thank you that my
life with you will last forever.

ADDITIONAL READING

Romans 8:17–18 • Psalm 136:1

Proverbs 18:10 • John 4:14

> "Do not be afraid; you will not be put to shame. Do not fear disgrace; you will not be humiliated. You will forget the shame of your youth and remember no more the reproach of your widowhood."
>
> ISAIAH 54:4

CONTEXT

The prophet Isaiah began his ministry in 740 BC, which was a time when Israel was in decline and Assyria was a constant threat as it grew into an empire. Isaiah's name means "the Lord saves," which is fitting since the themes of the book are God's judgment and salvation.

MEANING

Chapter 54 of Isaiah is a call of encouragement to Israel, comparing the nation to a barren, abandoned woman who will soon be fruitful. Being childless in those days was a great shame for a woman. But God himself would be her husband! He says he was punishing Israel for a time, while always knowing that time would end and would be followed by a relationship that would last forever. God promises "everlasting kindness" and "unfailing love."

Verse 4 of this chapter is a specific call—perhaps it could even be considered a commandment—not to be afraid. But this call by God is about a very specific kind of fear—the fear of being ashamed or humiliated. In the context of this chapter, this shame was being experienced by Israel in the presence of their surrounding enemies. They may have been ashamed of their own weakness, small size, and perhaps even of the God they'd worshiped. They were face-to-face with Assyria, a powerful, sophisticated enemy that was marching through that part of the world, taking over any nations standing in its way. And now God was asking them not to fear being disgraced.

Not fearing can be an act of obedience. When God tells us not to fear, he of course wants us to rest and find peace in him. But he also wants us to step out in faith. It's a command and an expectation, which means it can be obeyed. The verse is implying that in some way we have control of our emotions and can lean into our faith in God and away from fear.

APPLICATION

Do you treat fear as something God wants you to reject? Can you decide to trust that God has your back and will not lead you into shame? There is no humiliation for those who put their faith in him.

But just because we can decide not to fear doesn't mean it's easy, or that we can do it on our own. Ask God for his strength to overcome fear. And trust that he will hear your prayer.

ADDITIONAL READING

2 Timothy 1:6–8 • Romans 10:11–12

> "Then Jesus declared, 'I am the bread of life. Whoever comes to me will never go hungry, and whoever believes in me will never be thirsty.'"
>
> JOHN 6:35

CONTEXT

The book of John was written by the apostle John, one of Jesus' closest friends during his earthly ministry. It is believed that this was the last of the Gospels to be written. The emphasis of John is on who Jesus is and how we can be saved through him.

MEANING

The sixth chapter of John begins with two of Jesus' most well-known miracles. The first is the feeding of five thousand, which brought great popularity to Jesus and his ministry. The second is his walking on water. Both of these miracles show that Jesus is God's Son, and he has complete power over all creation.

But while these are important signals of who Jesus is, they are not the reason he came. Jesus came to give eternal life to all who put their faith in him, and the central portion of this chapter is dedicated to that message. In fact, Jesus tells his listeners, "Do not work for food that spoils [the loaves and fishes], but for food that endures to eternal life, which the

Son of Man will give you. For on him God the Father has
placed his seal of approval" (John 6:27).

That's where verse 35 comes into play. Jesus is the bread
of life. He doesn't just provide the bread—that bread is him.
Without him there is no life. And how do we get this bread?
We come to Jesus in faith. In fact, this verse equates coming
to Jesus with believing in him. We come to him by calling
out to him in faith.

Jesus goes on to say, "This bread is my flesh, which I will
give for the life of the world." Jesus knows the sacrifice he
will make to give life to us, and yet he doesn't run from
the responsibility. Instead, he invites all to participate in
his sacrifice, eating his flesh and drinking his blood. These
are gruesome images (you can imagine how they must have
sounded to his listeners). But Christ's death was gruesome
indeed. Sin is no joke.

He welcomes all to come to him to accept this sacrifice on
our behalf. And when we do, eternal life is ours.

APPLICATION

Come to Jesus. Believe in him. This is the only path to eternal life. But coming to Jesus isn't a one-time thing for salvation. He is always there, loving us and providing life for us.
He who gave himself for you loves you eternally and wants
you to come to him with your needs, your fears, and your desires. You can trust him.

ADDITIONAL READING

Romans 10 • Exodus 16:4

> "So God created mankind in his own
> image,
>   in the image of God he created
>   them;
> male and female he created them."
>
> GENESIS 1:27

CONTEXT

The book of Genesis is believed to have been written by
Moses while in the wilderness during Israel's wandering
years between Egypt and the promised land. If there was
one key verse to summarize the book of Genesis as a whole,
it would be this one. The fact that we are created in the
image of the almighty God should bring about a deep-rooted
humility, as well as an unshakable confidence in the unmer-
ited love of our Father. This is the posture that we should
diligently maintain as we navigate life as followers of Christ.

MEANING

This verse in Genesis sets the stage for all of Scripture with
mankind as children of God. We are not subjects, peasants,
or slaves. We are God's children. And because he is good in
nature and perfect in love, he takes care of our every need.
However, this means that sometimes he must withhold what
we want. For example, a child wants to be rescued by Dad
when a bully threatens to cause harm. But the good father

recognizes that it is only in the face of such a threat that a child can learn to overcome the fear of the situation to exemplify the love and strength that his father has taught him. Similarly, the faithful child recognizes the object of the lesson and faces the test with humility and confidence, drawing strength from the fact that the father is watching ever so closely and would never leave him.

APPLICATION

Worry is a natural byproduct resulting from the uncertainty of life. But we, as followers of Christ, have something that the rest of the world does not: the knowledge that God is watching us ever so closely and that he will never leave us. Is there a threat that you are having to face down? I encourage you to recognize the object of the lesson. Draw strength from the Lord as you work to exemplify him in the face of your opposition. Approach each day with humility and confidence. Study the character of your Father and work to emulate him. This way, when opposition looks at you, it sees the image of the almighty God, and retreats.

ADDITIONAL READING

James 1:2–4 • Matthew 10:19 • Matthew 6:25–34

> " 'No weapon forged against you will prevail, and you will refute every tongue that accuses you. This is the heritage of the servants of the Lord, and this is their vindication from me,' declares the LORD."
>
> ISAIAH 54:17

CONTEXT

The prophet Isaiah began his ministry in 740 BC, which was a time when Israel was in decline and Assyria was a constant threat as it grew into an empire. Isaiah's name means "the Lord saves," which is fitting since the themes of the book are God's judgment and salvation.

MEANING

We looked at chapter 54 of Isaiah earlier in this book, specifically at verse 17 and its promise that no weapon forged against you will prevail. As mentioned then, this chapter is a message of encouragement to Israel, comparing the nation to a barren, abandoned woman who will soon be fruitful.

Verse 17 is a powerful conclusion to this chapter, letting us know that God protects his servants. There is no weapon of the enemy—whether the enemy is spiritual or physical—that can overcome those under God's care. All your enemies' accusations will come to nothing. God is the creator of all, and he has everything under control. Your suffering, whatever it may be, is temporary. But God's love and peace is eternal.

The apostle Paul quotes this chapter in his letter to the Galatians, which indicates that this is not just a promise to Israel. He uses it to talk about believers as "children of promise." If you put your trust in Christ, you are God's servants and his children.

APPLICATION

While in the middle of a battle—whether it's a physical battle, a spiritual battle, a relationship battle, or something else—it is important to assess the strength of both sides. Your enemy may be strong, but God is infinitely stronger. Take courage in the fact that nothing happens without God's permission, and that in the end, he promises his everlasting kindness and unfailing love. Pray these promises back to him and claim them for your own.

ADDITIONAL READING

Galatians 4　•　Isaiah 55

> "... he saved us, not because of
> righteous things we had done,
> but because of his mercy. He saved
> us through the washing of rebirth
> and renewal by the Holy Spirit."
>
> TITUS 3:5

CONTEXT

The book of Titus was written by the apostle Paul to Titus, his friend and colleague in ministry. The letter was sent while Titus was leading a new church on the island of Crete, and it gives guidance about issues of church organization and how to live a godly life, as well as warnings against false teaching.

MEANING

Chapter 3 of Titus begins with wise instruction about how to conduct yourself in culture and society: Be humble and obedient to authority, live in peace, don't lie about others, be gentle. While our cultural context is always changing, these wise words remain as a guide for what the Christian life should look like.

The chapter goes on to contrast this lifestyle to the way the believers lived before they knew Christ. They were foolish and disobedient and easily deceived, "enslaved by all kinds of passions and pleasures," and lived with hatred and envy. This is what we were like before Christ came to save us. He didn't show mercy to good people, but to evil ones.

Which brings us to our focal verse. Our salvation had nothing to do with anything we'd done, but was an act of mercy by a loving God. Through his grace we were born again and renewed by the Holy Spirit. We are no longer what we used to be. In other words, there is a powerful turning point in the life of every Christian. When you trust Christ, you become a new creature. You were once at war with God, and now you are in his family.

From there, Paul goes on to talk about our new lives as heirs of God's kingdom. But with that privilege comes the responsibility to live up to our new position. Do what is good and avoid arguments and divisiveness.

APPLICATION

Isn't it a wonder to know that your hope in Christ has nothing at all to do with what you've done? We often feel pressure to perform, feeling shame from our past, and that we aren't doing enough in the present. But this isn't the truth. That's not how the God of mercy works.

Admit to God that you're not good enough, that you can never earn his love. But thank him for loving you anyway. Then, place your trust in this God who loved you even in your evil state, who will withhold no good thing from you.

ADDITIONAL READING

Ephesians 2:8–10 • Galatians 5:16–26

> "Therefore, since we have been
> justified through faith, we
> have peace with God through
> our Lord Jesus Christ."
>
> ROMANS 5:1

CONTEXT

As mentioned earlier, the book of Romans is a letter written by the apostle Paul to the Christians living in Rome. Scholars believe he wrote it from Corinth and had never visited Rome before. The main reason for the letter was to give the new believers there a clear understanding of the basics of the Christian faith, the gospel, and the Christian's identity and responsibilities in Christ.

MEANING

This verse begins with a *therefore*, which means it is the conclusion to an argument. So what is the argument Paul makes in the previous chapter? It is that justification (our being made right with God) is not the result of our good works, but of faith. Abraham, the father of our faith, wasn't justified because he did good things for God, but because he trusted in God's promises. So too with us.

Chapter 5, then, goes on to describe what being "justified" means for us. What are the promises we can cling to when we're saved through faith in Christ? It all starts with peace. When we were not right with God, we had no peace.

We were not on the same side as the creator of the universe, so everything was wrong. But once our sins are forgiven and we are on God's side, we have access to the peace we've been longing for.

But it doesn't end with peace. The chapter goes on to describe how we have access to grace and to God's glory. Even our sufferings now have purpose—they produce perseverance, character, and hope.

None of this—hope, grace, peace, purpose—is possible without being justified through faith in Christ.

APPLICATION

The gospel of Jesus—our being brought into a relationship with God through Christ's death for our sins—is the basis of any peace we could ever hope for. Without that, everything else falls apart. But with that, nothing is wasted. Stand strong in the hope of the gospel today! Remind yourself that Jesus loved you enough to die for you, and therefore you have access to a peace that will last forever. Trouble will come, but it is temporary and will serve to prepare you for a glorious future.

ADDITIONAL READING

Romans 8:31–39 • Genesis 15:1–6

> "Now faith is confidence in
> what we hope for and assurance
> about what we do not see."
>
> HEBREWS 11:1

CONTEXT

The author of Hebrews is unknown, but it is likely the audience was Jewish Christians.

The author spent the previous chapters showing Jesus Christ as the Son of God, revealing God's plan of grace and salvation.

MEANING

Jesus is the promised Messiah, both High Priest going before the Father on our behalf and the final sacrificial lamb to take away the sins of the world once and for all. We no longer rely on an earthly priest or animal sacrifice of the Jewish tradition, but we now have faith and "confidence to enter the Most Holy Place by the blood of Jesus" (10:19). We know our sins are washed away. We are forgiven and now have access to God the Father and his very presence. This is our assurance of salvation and faith. Faith is not a vague feeling or concept, but a rooted confidence in who Christ is and a trust that God is who he says he is, and that his promises will come to pass.

APPLICATION

It is easy to know that the right thing to do is trust God and have faith, but why can we trust and have faith?

As a son and daughter of God, your hope, your confidence, and your faith must be rooted in Christ. Then, in every circumstance, you have the opportunity to respond out of that restful, settled assurance of what you already know—the good news, the promises, and the character of our mighty God. If we can reassess circumstances in the light of this assurance, we can begin to walk in hope.

Pray the Lord reminds you to focus on who he is, and what he has already done to make a way for you. Let this assurance of your salvation and his unending faithfulness come alive in your heart and mind.

God has called us, so we need not lose heart. We can confidently run the race because he knows what is ahead of us. He is trustworthy and good. He will "never leave us or forsake us" and "his mercies are new every morning."

ADDITIONAL READING

Deuteronomy 31:6 • Philippians 1:6 • Psalm 51:12

"But blessed are those who trust in the LORD and have made the LORD their hope and confidence. They are like trees planted along a riverbank, with roots that reach deep into the water. Such trees are not bothered by the heat or worried by long months of drought. Their leaves stay green, and they never stop producing fruit."

JEREMIAH 17:7–8 NLT

CONTEXT

In the chapter leading up to this verse, God is telling Jeremiah about the nation of Judah. The people of Judah had followed in their ancestors' footsteps, becoming unfaithful and abandoning God in favor of idols. And so, because of their insistence on following their own evil desires and their refusal to listen to him, God let them go. He left them to their ways, even though he knew they would waste away without him. But what could he do? They had their heart set and would not be turned from it. Instead of trusting in God, they decided to trust in their own ways.

MEANING

The result wasn't a thriving life. God compared them to stunted shrubs living in a barren, salty, uninhabited wilderness, without hope for the future. They were missing out on their best possible life.

But those who put their confidence in God? They are like trees planted along a riverbank, whose leaves stay green and never stop producing fruit. Even in hard seasons, when everything around them is drying up, their leaves are green because they are connected to a source of life that is unaffected by the seasons. Their lives are vibrant! They are fruitful, offering sustaining fruit to those around them. Not only are they fruitful in the fertile seasons of warmth and plentiful rain, but in all seasons.

APPLICATION

We were never meant to live dependent on our own strength and abilities, apart from God. That was never his plan for us. We were made to live in relationship with God, trusting him to guide us through and provide for us at each of life's twists and turns.

Whatever comes your way today, count on God. Instead of trusting in your own knowledge and logic, be confident in his reliability, his truth, his ability, and his strength. When we accept God's deep love for us, and we spend time studying his Word and learning his Truths, we will flourish. He will keep us thriving and vibrant through all of life's trials.

ADDITIONAL READING

Psalm 37:4 • John 10:10 • Jeremiah 29:11

> "Therefore, since we are surrounded by such a great cloud of witnesses, let us throw off everything that hinders and the sin that so easily entangles. And let us run with perseverance the race marked out for us."
>
> HEBREWS 12:1

CONTEXT

Just before this passage is what's known as "The Hall of Faith," leading us through a lightning-fast history of the Old Testament. The author has spent the first part of Hebrews encouraging believers to "hold fast" to their faith even in the midst of false teaching and persecution (10:23). The brief profiles in chapter 11 answer the question, "Who are the great cloud of witnesses?" mentioned in 12:1—they include people like Abraham and Moses and Rahab, who put their belief in God's promises into action.

MEANING

If you're like most of us, during times of suffering and struggle, fears whisper in the back of your mind when you're lying awake at night. Things like "No one understands," "I can't make it through this," "I'm completely alone" creep in.

The great comfort of this verse is that God understands, and he lovingly responds by telling you three things: you're not alone, the weight you're feeling is real, and the goal is always worth the struggle it takes to get there.

The image of a race is one that stands the test of time. Even back in ancient Greece when these verses were written, races had several key components: there was a crowd watching and cheering, athletes had to persevere through obstacles and weariness, and a finish line met the runners at the end.

Like a race, the Christian life has a "cheering section"— our brothers and sisters in Christ who have dealt with many of the same trials and temptations we do. Just like marathon runners training for their goal, this life isn't going to be easy, but when sin and selfishness threaten to distract us, we can push those things aside and move forward. Victory is already ours in Jesus . . . so let's keep running!

APPLICATION

Think about the obstacles that might be holding you back from spiritual growth. Are there any distractions that might "hinder" you from focusing on God? Maybe it's a bad habit or attitude you find yourself slipping into, like grumbling or gossip, or maybe there's something other than God you look to for hope and fulfilment. What sin "easily entangles" you? Is there a Scripture you could use to fight back when temptation comes? Like staying physically fit, focusing on running your spiritual race well takes effort, but you can take comfort in knowing that you'll never have to go through a difficult season alone.

ADDITIONAL READING

1 Corinthians 9:24–25 • Acts 20:24 • 2 Timothy 4:7

> "Consider it pure joy, my brothers
> and sisters, whenever you
> face trials of many kinds."
>
> JAMES 1:2

CONTEXT

The book of James is a call to action for believers to ensure their faith is authentic and to produce word and deed accordingly. James 1:22 says believers shouldn't just *listen* to the Word, but that we should actually *do* what it says. The first chapter begins the call by addressing our reaction to trials and our response to hearing the Word of God.

MEANING

Trials are inevitable in our lives. James talks about *when* we experience trials, not *if* we experience trials. However, our reaction may uncover the state of our faith. James asks us to "consider it a pure joy" when disruptions come our way. Joy likely isn't our natural response to adversity. Why then would James instruct us to view it as such? James 1:3 holds the answer: "Because you know that the testing of your faith produces perseverance." The authenticity of our faith is revealed when it's tested, and the more difficulties we face, the stronger our faith will grow. If we never encounter trouble, our faith may lack a secure foundation. Trials refine our faith and strengthen our character. This is why we should accept life's disruptions with joy and view them as opportunities to walk closer with Jesus.

Abundant spiritual growth can come from adversity, but if we don't posture our hearts correctly before Jesus, we will miss the opportunity. Grab hold of these opportunities to draw closer to the Lord. Get on your knees and talk to your Father in heaven. He is there waiting to comfort you and to wrap his arms around you.

APPLICATION

When trials come your way, instead of asking "why me?" ask "why not me?" Jesus never promised that we would live free from difficulty. Actually, Jesus promised that we *would* live with difficulty. Use your trials as opportunities to produce stronger, richer faith and character. Use your trials to draw closer than ever to your Savior. Share your experiences with someone walking through a similar situation to offer comfort or advice. Ask Jesus to help you view these hard times as periods of joy, and ask him to refine your faith in the process.

ADDITIONAL READING

Isaiah 55:8–9 • Romans 5:3–5 • James 1:12

1 Peter 1:6–7 • 1 Peter 5:10

> "But you are a chosen people,
> a royal priesthood, a holy nation,
> God's special possession, that you
> may declare the praises of him
> who called you out of darkness
> into his wonderful light."
>
> 1 PETER 2:9

CONTEXT

First Peter is a letter written by the apostle Peter to the
Christians in several cities of modern-day Turkey. Peter was
one of Jesus' closest friends during his earthly ministry, and
after Jesus' resurrection, he became one of the most prominent leaders of the early church. The focal point of the letter
is Jesus Christ himself.

MEANING

The second chapter of this book begins by focusing the
Christian's attention on not being hateful or deceptive, but
instead focusing on Christ and his work on your behalf. From
there, Peter goes on to talk about those who reject Jesus ver-
sus those who accept him. Those who trust in him will never
be put to shame, whereas those who reject him will stumble
and fall.

Verse 9 digs deeper into who we are as believers. We are
chosen. We are royal. We are holy. We are owned by God.

What precious promises these are! To realize that the God of
the universe has chosen you as his own, and not only that but
lifted you up to the heights of royalty, is an astounding thing
to consider. Why would he do such a thing? In order to praise
him.

He called us from darkness into light, and he deserves our
praise. Not only does he deserve it, but it's good for us because that's what we were made for. In fact, if you hold back
your praise, you're the one who will be missing out, not God.

Immediately after this verse, Peter goes on to remind his
readers: You weren't always in this position. Once you were
without a community, and now you're in the community of
God. Once you were without mercy, but now he's given you
the mercy you needed.

APPLICATION

Being chosen is a wonderful thing. But we don't always feel
chosen, do we? We may get rejected by a friend, a romantic
interest, or an employer—rejection comes for us all at some
point in our lives.

But if you put your trust in Christ, you can rest assured
that God has chosen you. He knows your name and lifts you
up to a position of honor and royalty. The next time you're
feeling worried, praise God, because he has called you his
own and cares about your every need.

ADDITIONAL READING

John 15:15–17 • 2 Thessalonians 2:13–14

> "For you did not receive the spirit of slavery to fall back into fear, but you have received the Spirit of adoption as sons, by whom we cry, 'Abba! Father!'"
>
> ROMANS 8:15 ESV

CONTEXT

Chapter eight of Paul's letter to the Romans serves as a reminder that we have life in Christ Jesus. And when we have life in Jesus, we will never be separated from the Father, and he will love us forever—as his own children.

MEANING

The spirit of slavery is the reverse of God's character. Anything that God opposes, the spirit of slavery endorses. Jesus' death on the cross freed us from our bondage to sin. Therefore, we have also been set free from fear: fear of the unknown, of illnesses, of loss, and certainly of death. All of the earthly concerns we have, Jesus has already defeated.

By our faith in Jesus' death and resurrection, God has adopted us as his own children. Jesus' love for us is so great that he made us co-heirs with him. We are not just acquaintances of God; we are not his neighbor or even his dear friend. We are his children, his sons and his daughters. We even get to call him "Abba, Father."

No matter what circumstances you find yourself facing today, remember that Jesus has already won favor for you, a child of God. Yes, there is still suffering in that. Actually, just a few verses later, Paul reminds us that "we suffer with him in order that we may also be glorified with him" (Romans 8:17). Your suffering, the worry and anxiety that you feel, is not in vain when your heart is pointed toward the Father. You are God's child; find rest in your Father.

APPLICATION

Don't you wish you could drop everything, walk upstairs into your Father's room, and just sit in his presence for a while, knowing that his wisdom far exceeds your problems? Go grab your Bible, head to a comfortable spot in your home, and turn to your favorite passage. What do you learn about God on that page? Maybe you'll be reminded of his grace, his mercy, his sovereignty, or that "in him all things hold together" (Colossians 1:17). Let that wisdom wash over you while you meditate on your verse.

God is your Father. When your anxiety seems like too much to handle, remember who he is, and let that knowledge comfort you. God didn't put you in your situation alone. He called you to be his child and lets you cry, "Abba!"

ADDITIONAL READING

1 Corinthians 2:12 • Galatians 4:6 • 2 Timothy 1:7

> "So don't worry about tomorrow,
> for tomorrow will bring its
> own worries. Today's trouble
> is enough for today."
>
> MATTHEW 6:34 NLT

CONTEXT

This verse comes from Jesus' Sermon on the Mount, which can be found in Matthew 5–7. In this section of the sermon, Jesus is teaching the crowds about money, possessions, and worry. In chapter 6:25 (NLT) he says, "That is why I tell you not to worry about everyday life—whether you have enough food and drink, or enough clothes to wear. Isn't life more than food, and your body more than clothing?" Then in verse 27 he continues with, "Can all your worries add a single moment to your life?"

MEANING

What Jesus is saying here is that God can provide for even our most basic needs for life. And if he is able to do that, what can't he do? He is able to work in impossible ways. He is also able to work in ways we would never expect! Because he holds the world in his hands, he instructs us to think about only today. And even in light of today, we should not worry. Instead, he instructs us to seek the kingdom of God above all else, live righteously, and as we do so, he will give us everything we need.

The charge for you today is to think only about today. Be aware of the decisions you're making and how they impact the days to come. The way you handle today will affect tomorrow. Healthy thought patterns and habits don't just happen "one day." Rather, they are a collective culmination of our seemingly simple daily choices. Learning to follow Christ and to trust him is a daily discipline.

APPLICATION

So what can you do today? You can trust that God is faithful to come through when you depend on him. You can pray throughout the day, believing that he's listening. You can choose to fill your mind with things of God instead of things of this world.

Jesus told us that in this life we'll face many hardships, but he also promised to be with us every step of the way. So today, focus on that truth that "he is with us." May hope in Christ be your anchor today, keeping you steady through the waves.

ADDITIONAL READING

Joshua 1:9 • Psalm 46:1 • James 1:2–4

> "Praise be to the God and
> Father of our Lord Jesus Christ,
> who has blessed us in the
> heavenly realms with every
> spiritual blessing in Christ."
>
> EPHESIANS 1:3

CONTEXT

Ephesians is a letter written by the apostle Paul to the church at Ephesus, which was a city in modern-day Turkey. The primary purpose of the letter is to teach and reinforce the major themes of the gospel.

MEANING

After a brief greeting of grace and peace to the believers at Ephesus, Paul jumps right in to a message of encouragement, praising God for his blessings on those who trust in Christ. So what, exactly, does that blessing entail? First, he chose us to become his children before the world was even created. Second, he redeemed us, paying for our sins through the blood of his Son, Jesus Christ. And finally, he revealed this plan to us, making us part of his unified kingdom and giving us the Holy Spirit as a guarantee of our adoption as his children.

Verse 3 says that we are blessed with "every spiritual blessing in Christ," but when Paul goes on to explain what that means, he focuses on our adoption into God's family. Why is that? Because there is no greater blessing than being a child of God. Whatever you're longing for—health, healing of relationships, financial security, etc.—will all come to an end when you die. Without the eternal life that can only be found in Christ, everything is temporary and therefore is not as valuable as it seems in this world. But in Christ we live forever in his grace and peace. And as it says in Matthew, "all these things will be given to you as well" (6:33). In other words, as God's sons and daughters, we have access to everything God has—which is *everything*. As verse 4 of Ephesians 1 reminds us, he is the creator of the world. What could we possibly want that he doesn't have? And as his adopted children, all of creation is our inheritance as well.

APPLICATION

Are you a child of God? If not, you are invited into his family by trusting in Christ for the forgiveness of your sins. And if you are his child, remind yourself of that when you pray. In fact, that is why Jesus began the Lord's Prayer with "Our Father . . ." We are to come to him as his children. That means in humility (we're not the parent in this relationship), but also in boldness (we aren't a stranger asking a favor).

ADDITIONAL READING

Romans 8:14–17 • Matthew 6:28–34

> "Glory to God in the highest heaven, and on earth peace to those on whom his favor rests."
>
> LUKE 2:14

CONTEXT

The Gospel of Luke was written by a Gentile doctor who traveled with Paul on some of his missionary journeys. Luke wrote the book to Theophilus, who many believe was a wealthy Roman official, in order to give him an account of Jesus' life and ministry and show the way of salvation.

MEANING

Luke chapter 2 is the fullest account of Jesus' birth story in the Bible. It begins with an explanation of why Mary and Joseph have to travel to Bethlehem (for tax reasons), and how there is no room for them there. This is why they have to settle into a stable.

In verse 8, the scene shifts to a field nearby, where shepherds are watching their flocks under the stars. An angel shows up, revealing God's glory. This understandably terrifies the shepherds, but immediately the angel reassures them that he has good news for them rather than judgment. He tells them where to find a baby that will be their Messiah and Lord.

The angel is joined by a huge number of other angels, filling the skies with the song we read above. The lyrics of the song they sing can be summarized as: 1) God is worthy of all glory; and 2) he wishes peace for us.

What a brief but powerful message. How can sinners like us have peace with a glorious, perfect God? That is the question behind the gospel message. And the first step for the gospel to be fulfilled was for Christ to come in human form, as a baby.

APPLICATION

God is glorious. God wants peace with us. If we read only the first line, we worship God in terror. If we emphasize only the second line, we can fall into the trap of not truly acknowledging God's holiness, which takes away the whole point of being saved from our sins.

But when we put these two things together, they paint a complete picture of a perfect God who also wants to be in a relationship with us. There is no better news than this! When you're not at peace, remind yourself that God is on your side. He wants there to be peace in your mind and heart. The next step is to ask him to help you get there, which can only happen through Christ's sacrifice for you.

ADDITIONAL READING

Romans 5:1–5 • Colossians 1:19–20

> "Every good gift and every
> perfect gift is from above, coming
> down from the Father of lights,
> with whom there is no variation
> or shadow due to change."
>
> JAMES 1:17 ESV

CONTEXT

The book of James is often referred to as wisdom literature, much like what we see from the Old Testament's Psalms, Proverbs, and Ecclesiastes. James was indeed wise, writing with complete acceptance of Christian doctrine and exercising his religion with the first-century church in Jerusalem. Paul dubbed James a pillar of the church in Galatians 2:9. This is to say, James has an authority that lends us the ability to trust his message. He was no doubt aware of and fell subject to the persecution Christians would have suffered during this time in history. Worry, fear, and anxiety would have been common emotions for James and his fellow believers, and well-warranted.

MEANING

And yet, James exhorts us to remember that we have a high spiritual goal, and to be on guard against falling victim to the pressures that surround us; we're called to walk in faith and to evidence our transformation in Christ by exhibiting good works. Through belief and obedience, God gives what we need to live this way. In his unfailing consistency, he gives us good and perfect gifts! Some like to differentiate between "good gifts," i.e., earthly provisions from the Lord such as health, relationships, work, and sustenance—even the ability to read this book!—while others like to call out the "perfect gifts," which are spiritual and eternal gifts such as redemption, forgiveness, regeneration, and salvation. Hallelujah!

APPLICATION

When encumbered with difficulty—be it from outside ourselves through circumstances, or from inside ourselves through struggles with behavior or conscience—God desires to give us his good gifts. Noticeable signs of struggle, such as emotions like worry and anxiety, can be assuaged when we go to the Lord and ask him to show us our good and perfect gifts. We could keep a running tally for our own reference. And when the list seems complete, we could ask the Lord if he has any new gifts he would like to impart on or in us. Worries and anxieties will come, but the Lord has gifts for us to handle them. We must merely ask.

ADDITIONAL READING

Matthew 7:9-11 • John 14:3 • John 16:33

Ephesians 2:8 • Colossians 1:27

> "Pray like this: Our Father in heaven,
> may your name be kept holy."
>
> MATTHEW 6:9 NLT

CONTEXT

This verse comes to us from Jesus' famous Sermon on the Mount, which begins in Matthew chapter 5. With his disciples gathered around him, Jesus sat down on the mountainside and began teaching the crowds that had come to hear him teach. In this sermon, he covered a wide range of topics, from Jewish law, to anger, giving to the needy, prayer, and more.

MEANING

Jesus started his teaching about prayer in Matthew 6:5. Here, he explains that prayer is an intimate conversation we have with our Father. And even though God knows exactly what we need even before we ask him, he still wants us to intentionally bring our needs and requests to him. So he instructs us to get out of the public eye and hide ourselves away in a quiet, private place. When we hide ourselves away, Jesus tells us that we can be confident that God sees us and is listening. Then, as we pray, we are to recognize and acknowledge that our Father is in heaven. He is not bound by earthly rules. He is not influenced by worldly trends or politics. He is outside of everything and able to accomplish infinitely more than we could ask or think (Ephesians 3:20).

APPLICATION

Hiding away in a quiet, solitary place to pray may appear insignificant. It may even feel too simple, as though no power could possibly come from such an unseen, quiet action. But the very opposite is true. It is there that God, who calls himself your heavenly Father, wishes to meet with you. He comes down from heaven, all the way into your hidden, secluded space, just to listen to your prayers.

Right now, go into that private place and tell God what is on your mind or heavy on your heart. While you do so, remind yourself of who he is. He is the creator of everything, he is the redeemer of your soul, and he is the author and perfecter of your faith. He is God, who longs to meet with you.

Give him all of it. He wants to hear it. Trust Jesus' words that your Father knows exactly what you need, and that he sees everything.

ADDITIONAL READING

Hebrews 11:3 • Philippians 4:19–20 • Psalm 16:7–8

> " '[Teach] them to observe all
> that I commanded you; and
> behold, I am with you always,
> to the end of the age.' "
>
> MATTHEW 28:20 NASB

CONTEXT

After his death and resurrection, Jesus appeared to his disciples many times over the course of forty days. He taught them and ate and drank with them, but most important, he gave them a task—to preach the gospel to every person in every town and country in the world. This task is known as the Great Commission, and it's something all Christians are called to do.

MEANING

God has always been in the business of telling humans the good news about himself. For thousands of years, God commissioned prophets, priests, and leaders to remind people of his love and kindness, and to warn them of the coming punishment should they continue in their evil and sinful ways.

But humans are born evil—wanting to follow their own hearts and desires instead of God's. Over the years, many prophets, priests, and leaders who have come declaring God's message to the world have been jeered at, scorned, tortured, maimed, hated, driven from their homes, and disowned by

their families. Some were even executed, sometimes in grue-
somely creative ways.

Jesus' disciples knew this history of persecution, and Jesus
himself even said that "a prophet has no honor in his own
country" (John 4:44). Nevertheless, God uses people to declare the good news about himself and the salvation all may
receive through believing in Jesus' life, death, and resurrection. And God isn't going to change his tactics.

But Jesus also knew that these missionaries he was com-
missioning to spread the good news about him would face
many horrible things—stonings, being worshiped as "gods,"
exile, execution—so he did not ascend into heaven without
leaving them with comfort and a promise to cling to. Wherever they would go, whatever wonderful and horrible things
they would surely face, Jesus promised to be with them always, from that moment and into eternity.

APPLICATION

Just like the twelve disciples, Christians today are called to
tell everybody about Jesus. And just like the Twelve, we will
all experience some kind of persecution. Some may lose their
jobs, their families, or even their lives. Others may be slan-
dered or hated by their neighbors. Even so, we have a sure
foundation in Christ, and we have his promise to cling to.
As we proclaim the good news of Jesus to the world, he will
never leave us or forsake us. He knows that following this
commission is hard, and he will be with us every step of the
way—from the moment we're saved and throughout eternity.

ADDITIONAL READING

Joshua 1:9 • Isaiah 41:10 • 1 Chronicles 22:18

2 Corinthians 4:7–18

"Finally, brothers and sisters,
whatever is true, whatever is
noble, whatever is right, whatever
is pure, whatever is lovely,
whatever is admirable—if anything
is excellent or praiseworthy—
think about such things."

PHILIPPIANS 4:8

CONTEXT

The book of Philippians was a letter written by the apostle
Paul to Christians in the Roman city of Philippi. Paul wrote
it while he was in prison for his faith, and yet the themes
of the letter are gratitude, encouragement, and joy. He was
thankful to God, of course, but also to the Philippians for the
kindness they had shown him.

MEANING

Paul, who was on trial for his life, was not willing to give in
to fear. Christ had rescued him from sin and had given him
peace and joy, so Paul refused to let his circumstances dis-
courage him.

Philippians 4:8 is about focusing our hearts and minds.
While we are not in control of the world around us, we can
direct our thoughts toward the things of God. That means

choosing not to dwell on what is wrong but instead turning our attention to what is right. It means not focusing on the bad things that might happen, but rather reminding ourselves that we serve a powerful God who has everything in his hands. There are always things to be thankful for, we just have to learn to see them.

We've already talked about verses 6 and 7 of chapter 4, which instruct the Philippians not to be worried about anything, but to pray and be thankful and let God's peace fill them. This gratitude and commitment to prayer are closely linked to the instructions in verse 8 about focusing our minds. From there, verse 9 asks them to remember all Paul has taught them, including how they've seen him live his life. In other words, he wasn't just telling them to dwell on good and praiseworthy things—he was showing them. He urged the believers in Philippi to follow his example.

APPLICATION

Focusing on the good, regardless of the concerns on your mind, is not easy. It takes effort and discipline, and of course you'll need God's help. Pray that God gives you reminders of all he's done for you throughout your day. This focus doesn't come naturally—it's usually easier to worry than to count your blessings—but it will get easier over time. As you exercise these mind muscles, they'll grow stronger.

And little by little, you'll discover that dwelling on the good things, the wholesome things, the praiseworthy things, will change you. Your heart will be filled with peace and joy, and when bad things come your way, you'll trust God more easily.

ADDITIONAL READING

Romans 12:2 • 2 Timothy 1:7 • Proverbs 4:23

> "For God so loved the world,
> that he gave his only Son, that
> whoever believes in him should
> not perish but have eternal life."
>
> JOHN 3:16 ESV

CONTEXT

In chapter 3 of the Gospel of John, a religious leader named Nicodemus comes to talk with Jesus at night, probably hoping he won't be seen. Jesus tells Nicodemus what it means to be born again, which causes Nicodemus to ask all kinds of questions. In what might be the most well-known verse of the Bible, Jesus explains why he came and how to have eternal life.

MEANING

Jesus tries to explain to Nicodemus what it means to be born again in several different ways. First, he says that to be born again means to be born of the Spirit rather than the flesh. Then he uses an illustration from the Old Testament.

As the Hebrews wandered in the desert, there was a time when they dealt with poisonous snakes. God told Moses to make a snake and place it on a pole. Anyone who had been bitten by a snake could look at the snake on the pole and live rather than die (Numbers 21). As a religious leader, Nicodemus would have been very familiar with these events. Jesus says to him, "And as Moses lifted up the serpent in the

wilderness, so must the Son of Man be lifted up, that whoever believes in him may have eternal life" (John 3:14–15
ESV).

Jesus was lifted up on a tree to die so that we might live
forever. He came to earth to show us God's great love for us
by dying for us. He loves us that much! And all we have to do
to have eternal life is look up to Jesus and believe in him.

APPLICATION

We tend to think that there must be a whole list of things to
check off before we're good enough to get into heaven: pray
every day, share our faith, be generous with our money, serve
at church—the list could go on and on. But in this verse,
Jesus told us all that is required.

Are you living as if you need to earn God's approval? Do
you feel as if you can never measure up? There's nothing
you can do to earn God's love or become worthy of heaven.
When you don't feel good enough, remember God's great
love for us. Remember that all he asks is that we believe in
Jesus.

ADDITIONAL READING

Joel 2:32 • John 6:29 • Romans 10:9

> " 'For I know the plans I have for you,'
> declares the Lord, 'plans to prosper
> you and not to harm you, plans
> to give you hope and a future.' "
>
> JEREMIAH 29:11

CONTEXT

This is a verse we all know well, right? Easily one of the most
encouraging verses in the Bible, we're sure to find it written
on most cards given during graduations, marriages, funerals.
What better words to reflect on when facing all the emotions
of major life transition? We can hold on to the promise that
the right college, right job, right spouse, right joy awaits us
just around the corner.

MEANING

For the Israelites in Jeremiah's time, the right thing was being
in Jerusalem. Both those who were left behind in the holy city
and those enslaved assumed that Jerusalem's overall prosperity was a sign of God's favor, and the ultimate goal was to
get back near the temple to join in it, as soon as possible. But
that promise wasn't fulfilled until seventy years later—long
after that generation was dead. In fact, Jeremiah speaks the
opposite—that to Jerusalem will go the judgment, and to the
exiles the fulfilment of God's plans. And even further, that
those in exile should focus on thriving where they are. "Seek
the peace and prosperity of the city to which I have carried

you into exile. Pray to the LORD for it, because if it prospers, you too will prosper" (29:7). The Israelites were being called to not sit and wait for the next right thing, nor for their rescue, but rather to lean into their suffering and anguish.

Theologian and author Russell Moore says many people believe this verse to be about God rubber-stamping our desires and inclinations, when instead, "The Book of Jeremiah is all about God disrupting his people's plans and upending his people's dreams."[*] To what end? That we could know Christ. For the Israelites' ultimate promise was a Messiah, one who would reconcile the world to God, who would bear the suffering and judgment of sin so people could freely have a relationship with the Father. So this verse is not about hoping in a success or blessing soon to come (though our God loves to give good gifts to his children), but rather learning to prosper in our present circumstance, with the sure knowledge God is with us.

APPLICATION

We are not alone. He knows our every suffering, and by walking through this time, by flourishing in the hope of Christ, we can come to know him better and be more like him. "Blessed are those whose ways are blameless, who walk according to the law of the LORD. Blessed are those who keep his statutes and seek him with all their heart" (Psalm 119:1–2).

ADDITIONAL READING

Numbers 6:24–26 • John 1:16–18 • Isaiah 41:10–12
---

[*] Russell Moore, "Does Jeremiah 20:11 Apply to You?" Russell Moore, June 28, 2017, https://www.russellmoore.com/2017/06/28/jeremiah-2911-apply/.

> "And we know that for those who love God all things work together for good, for those who are called according to his purpose."
>
> ROMANS 8:28 ESV

CONTEXT

In this section of Paul's letter, he acknowledges our suffering and says, "For I consider that the sufferings of this present time are not worth comparing with the glory that is to be revealed to us" (Romans 8:18 ESV). Here, Paul looks toward the future glory for God's children.

MEANING

If you're dealing with anxiety, you've probably been told "everything is going to be okay." These words are never ill-intentioned; people do not mean harm when they tell you this. However, this phrase doesn't help with your anxiety in the moment. It can even feel like a slap in the face. Don't they understand? Everything is not okay.

The apostle Paul is not here to quickly shake off hard times. In fact, Paul had recently been stoned for sharing the good news of Jesus Christ, so he gets it; life is not easy. But what he says here is true: "All things work together for good." Paul is not giving you his version of "it's okay." Paul is sharing the gospel!

When God calls you, when you love Christ, the Holy
Spirit dwells in you, and all things do work together for good
because God is good. It's safe to say that Jesus' death on the
cross entailed more suffering than we will face in our life-
times. Jesus took your pains, your worries, your anxiety, your
sin, and he died to free you from that suffering. He bore that
weight on the cross! When you have faith in him and are in
pursuit of him, he works all things together for good. You
may not see that today or tomorrow, but know that God is
working on behalf of those whom he has called.

APPLICATION

Spend time today worshiping the Lord for all he has given
you! Life is difficult, yes. But finding moments to celebrate
his glory is endlessly important. When you're feeling like
everything is not okay, and you can't see his good plan, a
little bit of worship can quickly remind you of his presence
and his goodness. So cry out "Hallelujah!" Sing your favorite
worship song and give him praise today.

ADDITIONAL READING

Colossians 1:17 • 1 Thessalonians 5:16–18 • Hebrews 1:3

> ## "For nothing will be impossible with God."
>
> LUKE 1:37 ESV

CONTEXT

The first chapter of Luke very fittingly lays the backdrop to Luke's account of Jesus' birth and life. He begins with Gabriel's visits to Zechariah, then to Elizabeth to announce the coming of John the Baptist. And Luke continues with Gabriel's visit to Mary to announce that she has been chosen among women. "For nothing will be impossible with God" was Gabriel's last statement to any of these three humans during this encounter, and it emphatically punctuated the news he brought—most significantly that Mary, a young virgin engaged to be married, was pregnant with the Messiah.

MEANING

It stands to reason that although Mary is favored of God and has humbly submitted to the Lord's will for her life, she would be worried about how all of this would work out. Luke doesn't offer the reader that morsel, but we know she was only human. She had to have been concerned with how to tell Joseph, her betrothed, and what he would undoubtedly think and plan to do. She would have to suffer the judgment and misunderstanding of all her family, of her entire community. Her whole world was turned upside down in a miraculous moment. This had never happened before. To anyone. Ever. Scary!

To her credit, Mary took Gabriel at his word: She believed. Mary knew the Lord had done this because she knew she hadn't. So she let the anxiety-causing details of the situation take a backseat to the Word of the Lord.

APPLICATION

Oh, that we would have that same resolve! If we could lean into the Word of the Lord and believe his promises—after all, nothing will be impossible with God; he is in charge of the really, really big and the very, very small—our burdens are not too much for him. He cares for the birds of the air and the flowers of the field. He calls the stars by name and counts the hairs on our heads. He holds us in the palm of his hand. The heavens are his throne, and the earth is his footstool. He owns the cattle on a thousand hills. How intently he cares for us and our worries and anxieties. Today we can release our encumbrances to the Lord, for whom nothing is impossible.

ADDITIONAL READING

Numbers 11:23 • Psalm 50:10 • Psalm 147:4

Proverbs 30:4 • Isaiah 66:1 • Matthew 6:24–34

Matthew 11:30 • Luke 12:7

> "I lift up my eyes to the mountains—
> where does my help come from?
> My help comes from the LORD,
> the Maker of heaven and earth."
>
> PSALM 121:1–2

CONTEXT

Psalm 121 is the second of the fifteen Songs of Ascents, which tradition suggests were sung by pilgrims as they journeyed up to Jerusalem to keep the annual feasts, and possibly by worshipers at Mount Zion as they ascended the steps of the temple. This encouraging psalm details God's caretaking and preservation throughout their lifetime, comforting not only to travelers but to all his people.

MEANING

To face difficulties with confidence, we must know not only the source of our help, but the quality and authority of it as well. And there is no better help to be found than that provided by our Creator.

The psalmist indicates that when he is in trouble, he looks up and away from his besetting problems ("I lift up my eyes") toward the mountains. Why the mountains? Because the hills of Jerusalem—and Mount Zion in particular, as the site of David's tabernacle and then the temple—represent the dwelling place of God on earth. The psalmist looks to God to rescue or assist him, and continues with a question and answer that clarify and emphasize exactly who provides his help: the Lord. This is followed by more clarity and more emphasis with his description as "the Maker of heaven and earth."

With the help of the Maker at hand, is there really a problem?

APPLICATION

When we are tempted to worry about a troubling situation, twisting ourselves into knots, trying to solve this issue or fix that one, we must choose to take our focus off the presenting problem and the created world, and turn our gaze toward God, our unseen Creator who nevertheless is "an ever-present help in trouble" (Psalm 46:1).

Instead of approaching problem solving as a horizontal endeavor, moving inward to ourselves or reaching outward to those people and resources on the same created plane we are, we can employ our vertical relationship with our Maker, releasing our cares and troubles upward in the form of prayers and petitions, breaking the plane as well as an often-frustrating cycle of anxiety and striving.

In turn, when the Lord, whom no foe can withstand, moves in a situation, he is doing so from the vantage point of one who sees the end from the beginning and who knows the inner workings as well as the outer.

After all, no one can troubleshoot like the Manufacturer.

ADDITIONAL READING

Joshua 1:5–7　•　Psalm 46:9–11　•　Jeremiah 32:17
2 Chronicles 20:4–6

"So then, since we have a great High Priest who has entered heaven, Jesus the Son of God, let us hold firmly to what we believe. This High Priest of ours understands our weaknesses, for he faced all of the same testings we do, yet he did not sin. So let us come boldly to the throne of our gracious God. There we will receive his mercy, and we will find grace to help us when we need it most."

HEBREWS 4:14–16 NLT

CONTEXT

The book of Hebrews was written to Jewish believers in Christ, encouraging them to remain faithful to Jesus rather than return to Judaism. The book shows that Jesus is greater than Moses, Aaron, angels, prophets, and priests. In this particular passage, the author of Hebrews lists the many ways that Jesus is superior to the Jewish high priests.

MEANING

Jesus is the ultimate High Priest. The Old Testament earthly high priest entered the most sacred part of the temple—the

Holy of Holies—to offer an animal as a sacrifice for the forgiveness of the sins of the Jewish people. But Jesus sacrificed himself rather than an animal, and he entered into the presence of God in heaven instead of the temple. The earthly high priest was a sinful man, while Jesus had no sin. The high priest had to offer a sacrifice once a year in order for the people's sins to be forgiven. But Jesus died for our sins once and for all.

The second part of this Scripture talks about how Jesus understands our weaknesses, because he had them too. Verse 15 says Jesus faced all the testings we do. Whatever your sin, whatever your struggle, Jesus knows how you feel. Because of this, he sympathizes with us and gives us mercy and grace. We can take our needs to the Father because the Son gives us access, even more access than the High Priest.

Not only did Jesus sacrifice himself for us, intervening on our behalf before the throne of God, but he understands our every weakness, sympathizes with us, and offers us mercy and grace. What a Savior!

APPLICATION

If you've ever felt that no one understands your struggles and temptations, you were wrong. Jesus knows. He knows how you feel, he knows what you're going through, and he knows how hard it is. Because of what he's done for us, you can boldly go to God's throne and receive his mercy and grace.

Whatever your difficulty, take it to the throne. Lay it at the feet of the One who knows how it feels. Give it to your perfect High Priest. He will provide understanding, forgiveness, and freedom.

ADDITIONAL READING

Hebrews 7:27 • 1 Corinthians 10:13 • 1 John 2:1

> ## "I can do all this through him who gives me strength."
> ### PHILIPPIANS 4:13

CONTEXT

The book of Philippians was written by the apostle Paul to the church at Philippi, which was a city in eastern Macedonia. Paul had visited Philippi more than once and seemed very close to the church there, calling them his "joy and crown." The main point of the letter was to give them updates and encourage them toward faithfulness and unity in Christ.

MEANING

This chapter of the epistle to the Philippians is full of gems—especially for those who struggle with anxiety and fear. It contains the famous verse "Be anxious for nothing," as well as the well-known passage encouraging Christians to focus their minds on whatever is true, good, pure, and beautiful.

Verse 13 is also extremely popular, as we see it proclaimed by athletes and celebrities and other Christians in the spotlight. As well it should be—it's a powerful message about trusting in the Lord rather than ourselves. But what should we take it to mean? Is it a promise that whatever we strive for—fame, health, sports championships, etc.—we can achieve through Christ's strength?

The verses preceding 13 provide some clarity. Verses 11 and 12 talk about knowing what it's like to be in need but learning to be content in all circumstances. Paul talks about sometimes being well-fed but at other times being hungry. Does that sound like someone who always gets what he wants? All of a sudden, verse 13 doesn't sound like it's about achievement or success, but rather about having the strength to carry through regardless. It's about Christ being that strength for us when we don't have strength in ourselves.

"Doing all this" is less about accomplishing big things and more about Christ strengthening us for whatever he has in store for our lives. There will be hardship, but Christ will be there to comfort you. There will be weakness, but he will provide strength. But in the end, there will be victory, and he will be its author.

APPLICATION

Philippians 4:13 is a victory cry, but maybe not in the way it's often interpreted. It's less a guarantee of success and more a promise of God providing what we need in all circumstances. Claim this promise, regardless of what you're going through. We need God's power every day. We don't always know what he has in store for us, but we know nothing surprises him and that he's big enough to see us through.

ADDITIONAL READING

Psalm 46:1–3 • 1 Timothy 6:6–11

> "They will have no fear of bad news;
> their hearts are steadfast,
> trusting in the LORD."
>
> PSALM 112:7

CONTEXT

Like Psalm 111, Psalm 112 is an acrostic poem, which means each line begins with successive letters of the Hebrew alphabet. It's unclear who wrote Psalm 112, but the message within it cannot be missed: A heart fixed on God is steady, no matter what comes our way.

MEANING

Because we don't know who wrote Psalm 112, it's hard to know precisely what "bad news" the author might have been referring to. But one thing is certain: No one—despite age, race, gender, or station in life—gets a pass when it comes to hard times. In fact, as Jesus tells us in John 16:33, "In this world you will have trouble." Not *might* have trouble, but *will*.

That can be a downer, but there's more that both Jesus and the author of Psalm 112 want us to know. When our hearts trust in God, we don't have to be afraid of bad news. The verse doesn't say, "If you have faith in yourself, you won't be afraid of bad news." It doesn't say, "If you take control of the situation, you won't be afraid of bad news."

It instructs us clearly to keep our chin up during bad-news times—gaze fixed steadily on the Lord. In his commentary, Matthew Henry calls this attitude a "settled spirit."

APPLICATION

Every morning, we wake up to some sort of bad news on
our television sets or in our iPhone notifications. A virus is
spreading. A shooter opened fire. A tornado struck.

Sometimes the bad news strikes closer to home. The
phone rings, and you find out your child has been in an ac-
cident. You didn't get the job. Your best friend found out she
has cancer.

All of it can leave us feeling afraid, discouraged, and filled
with anxiety.

Then comes along Psalm 112:7: "Have no fear of bad
news."

Could we live like that? Could we face each day with a
steadfast heart, trusting in the Lord, no matter what comes
our way?

None of us likes bad news. We have a preference for a
good-news kind of life. But Psalm 112 tells us that one of
the advantages of having faith in God is being able to stand
firm in the midst of trial. God guards the minds of those who
walk with him.

We have a Good News God for a Bad News Day.

The good news is that we don't walk alone.

The good news is that, even on days when we lose a battle,
Jesus has won the war.

The good news is that our souls are secure, even when our
bodies are weak.

The good news is that we don't have to be afraid of the
bad news.

ADDITIONAL READING

John 16:33 • Proverbs 4:20–22 • Hebrews 12:2

> "So do not be afraid of them,
> for there is nothing concealed
> that will not be disclosed, or hidden
> that will not be made known."
>
> MATTHEW 10:26

CONTEXT

Matthew, the author of this Gospel, was a former tax collector who left his work to follow Jesus, becoming one of Christ's twelve apostles. Tax collecting was a despised profession by the Jewish people, as it was a way to get rich at the expense of your fellow countrymen. Matthew's account of Jesus' life places an emphasis on the fulfilling of Old Testament promises and prophecies.

MEANING

This verse is in the middle of a long passage where Jesus gathers his twelve disciples (called "apostles" here for the first time) and sends them away with instructions on how to disciple others. He gives them power to heal and power over demons, and instructs them to proclaim the kingdom of heaven.

But much of this passage is a warning. They will be hated. He is sending them out as sheep among wolves. Even their families will turn against them. And perhaps worst of all, they won't be believed.

Not being believed can be so painful, whether you've been wrongly accused or are just trying to stand up for the truth

and no one's listening. It can be so disheartening to preach
what God has taught you only to be mocked or ignored. But
Jesus promised us this: In the end, the truth always wins out.
There is nothing hidden that will not be disclosed. There
is such a thing as truth, and it is found in Jesus. And Jesus
guarantees that in the end, he will win. Every knee shall bow
and every tongue confess that he is Lord.

How encouraging that your preaching is not in vain.

APPLICATION

Keep preaching what God lays on your heart, with all
love and humility. You may not see the fruit now, but fruit
will come. Don't assume you know the truth in every circumstance, but know that the truth in every domain—
relationships, work, politics, and of course the gospel—will
always eventually come to light.

The gospel is a public message, gloriously so! It is for
everyone, and God wants it proclaimed to the ends of the
earth.

ADDITIONAL READING

Romans 14:11 • 1 Peter 3:15–16

> "How abundant are the good
> things that you have stored up
> for those who fear you, that you
> bestow in the sight of all, on
> those who take refuge in you."
>
> PSALM 31:19

CONTEXT

The psalms—the Bible's collection of prayers and hymns—
are each inspired by God, but they were also individually
written by people experiencing the trials and emotions that
all humans face, and therefore serve to help us understand
and heal our emotions.

Psalm 31 was written by David for "the director of music."
That means it was intended to be sung publicly.

MEANING

Psalm 31 is a prayer to God in the midst of trouble. Verse
after verse, David asks for rescue, talks about the traps laid
out for him, and admits his anguish and loneliness. We don't
know what particular difficulty David was facing when he
wrote this psalm (he faced a lot of anguish in his life), but it is
clear that this was no minor frustration. He is in despair, his
life is in danger, and it seems like no one is on his side.

But the Lord is with him. David always comes back to the
one who will never leave him or forsake him. He experienced

God's faithfulness again and again, and he knows he can rely on it in this present crisis.

Psalm 31 is quoted in many other passages of Scripture, the most well-known being when Christ yielded up his life on the cross with the words, "Into your hands I commit my spirit." Jesus used this hymn of submission and trust when he was going through the very worst of his own trial.

And so can we. All of Scripture, and the psalms in particular, reveal a God who wants our faith but also our honesty. This publicly sung hymn does not shy away from revealing hardship and distress. But it also doesn't leave us there.

Thus, we get to verse 19, where the tone of the psalm changes. No longer does David dwell on all that is wrong, but instead he joyfully immerses himself in the goodness of God. How abundant are the blessings he's stored up for us! The future is in his hands, and it is good! He will bless us publicly, "in the sight of all," if we take refuge in him. What a promise. What hope we have in the God who loves us.

APPLICATION

Cry out to God today, letting him know the depths of your troubles. He can handle it. But don't leave things there. Move from that low place to the elevated state of proclaiming his goodness! It may be hard at first, but it will lead to healing.

ADDITIONAL READING

Psalm 91:3–8   •   Ephesians 1:3–6

> "Trust in the LORD with all your heart
> and lean not on your own
>   understanding;
> in all your ways submit to him,
> and he will make your paths
>   straight."

PROVERBS 3:5–6

CONTEXT

The book of Proverbs is one of the five books of wisdom, which also include Job, Psalms, Ecclesiastes, and Song of Songs. The Proverbs, many of which were "written" by King Solomon, are a collection of lessons and sayings that inspire readers to live lives guided by wisdom and a healthy fear of the Lord.

MEANING

The chapter begins with a father imploring his son not to forget the wise teachings he is sharing. All of the advice the father shares, whether it be how to win favor with both God and those around him or why he should honor God with his wealth, circle around what he shares in verse 5: "Trust in the Lord with all your heart and lean not on your own understanding."

At the center of all the father's advice, he implores his son to *trust in the Lord* above all else, and the wisdom this

father is passing on is not his own but from the heavenly
Father. It is by listening and leaning on God's instruction
that true peace and prosperity are possible for believers.
That is why the father tells his son not to "lean on his own
understanding" or to "be wise in his own eyes" as we are all
tempted to do, but to keep on the steady and true path laid
out by the Lord.

APPLICATION

The thesis of the book of Proverbs is laid out in the first
chapter: "The fear of the LORD is the beginning of knowledge, but fools despise wisdom and instruction" (v. 7).

All of us are prone to seek wisdom from many sources,
whether it is a book, an expert, or people we trust. While
we can all find good advice from our mentors and peers, we
should all seek God's instruction and counsel first and fore-
most. When we look to the Lord, his Word, and the wisdom
of the Holy Spirit within us, we can find guidance for our
everyday lives. The fruits of the Spirit and character modeled
by Christ teach us how to conduct ourselves and treat others,
and the parables throughout the Bible give us examples of
how to walk in godly wisdom. Ultimately, the heavenly Father is the true way maker, and he is trustworthy to guide us
with his lovingkindness.

ADDITIONAL READING

Jeremiah 17:7-8 • Psalm 37

> "For I am convinced that neither death nor life, neither angels nor demons, neither the present nor the future, nor any powers, neither height nor depth, nor anything else in all creation, will be able to separate us from the love of God that is in Christ Jesus our Lord."
>
> ROMANS 8:38–39

CONTEXT

The book of Romans was written by the apostle Paul, likely in AD 57 on his third missionary journey. It is a letter intended for the people of the church of Rome, which was mostly Gentile but probably also had a substantial Jewish minority. Paul really wanted to visit this church in person but had not been able to, so this letter is in preparation for his hoped-for eventual visit. Paul didn't personally know this church yet, so his letter focuses on the basics of the gospel: salvation from sin and righteousness through God's grace, both Jews and Gentiles.

MEANING

Paul has spent the first eight chapters of Romans talking about the need for salvation through Christ because of sin.

Those who have accepted this freedom from sin will gain righteousness through sanctification, and fully experience God's love. The argument Paul has been making is concluded here on a very triumphant note!

Paul's phrase "For I am convinced" tells us that he's speaking from his heart and his own experience. He has such strong confidence in the permanence of God's love that he wants to make sure all other believers fully understand the scope and power of God's love too. He's declaring to the church that God will never stop loving them, and his love can never be taken away from them, not by anything. To illustrate and solidify his point, he lists out all the possible things the Romans might worry could take God's love away from them. Paul's intention is clearly to cover all the bases here. This list can be taken both literally and figuratively. For example, "neither height nor depth" can mean nothing above us, like a storm in the sky, and nothing below us, like the waves in the sea, and it can mean no matter how low we go or feel or high we go or feel.

APPLICATION

Even at your most worried and anxious, nothing you dream up or imagine can come between you and God's love for you. No matter how lonely, attacked, or weak you feel, God still loves you just as much as he always has and always will. He is more powerful than anything and anyone else, and his love wins out over everything and everyone: the natural and the supernatural, the now and the later, the actions of others and even your own actions.

No matter how unloved and alone you feel, God's Word is crystal clear—you are never unloved and you are never alone. When your ever-changing feelings threaten to overwhelm you, you can fall back on the unchanging truth of God's promises that are never overwhelmed.

ADDITIONAL READING

Isaiah 41:10 • Ephesians 3:17b–19

Special thanks to the following contributors, who with love and great thoughtfulness helped to create the much-needed *100 Best Bible Verses to Overcome Worry and Anxiety*:

Hannah Ahfield
Jeff Braun
Chandler Carlson
Noelle Chew
Deirdre Close
Crystal Dill
Elizabeth Frazier
Patnacia Goodman
Serena Hanson
Sharon Hodge
Kristen Larson
Luke Larson
Jennifer Dukes Lee

Amy Lokkesmoe
Holly Maxwell
Ellen McAuley
Andy McGuire
Andrea Ralston
Raela Schoenherr
Stephanie Smith
Christy Stigen
Elisa Tally
Brooke Vikla
Carrie Vinnedge
Kaila Yim

www.ingramcontent.com/pod-product-compliance
Lightning Source LLC
Chambersburg PA
CBHW060753100426
42813CB00004B/793